Studies in

MARRIAGE AND THE FAMILY

Studies in

MARRIAGE AND THE FAMILY

ROBERT R. BELL, Editor

Temple University

THOMAS Y. CROWELL COMPANY, New York

Established 1834

First Printing, March, 1968
Second Printing, October, 1968
Third Printing, March, 1970

Library of Congress Catalog Card Number: 68—13377.
Designed by Judith Woracek Barry
Manufactured in the United States of America.

PREFACE

A strong interest in the study of the family was common to American sociology up to about the time of World War II. During that period, the interest was in the family itself as the major institution of society and in how the family was related to the rest of society. Furthermore, almost all theoretical formulations recognized the great importance of the family to any understanding of the social nature of man.

However, in the period since the end of World War II, the study of the family has been much less significant to American sociology than during the pre-World War II era. This changing stress probably has its basis in two general developments of sociology. First, various areas of specialization in sociology took on greater importance, such as minority groups, political sociology, etc.; and essentially new areas of specialization emerged, such as industrial sociology, society and mental illness, etc. Second, the study of the family came increasingly to be identified with various moralistic "how-to-do-it" approaches. These approaches, frequently presented under the guise of being authentic social science, were often primarily value prescriptions and behavioral imperatives. This group often passed off under the label of "sociology" such cliches as "sex before marriage is ugly and after marriage, beautiful"; "husbands and wives can resolve their problems by being honest and talking them out"; "there are no delinquent children, only delinquent parents."

However, during the post-World War II period, there have been a number of good studies that have contributed to the sociology of the family. In the eight studies presented in this book, all but one was carried out after the end of World War II. Of these seven, four were produced during the 1950's and three during the 1960's. It is my personal belief that the studies selected for inclusion in this collection are the best that have been done in the various areas covered by the sociological study of the family. These selected studies also represent a wide range of methodological and theoretical approaches.

It is sometimes difficult to select from an entire study of book length a single chapter that may be presented on its own. The guide for these selections was to use what seemed to stand on its own, while continuing to give a fairly complete indication of the findings in the entire book. It is hoped that some readers may want to look at the entire book after reading the excerpt. Or, if an interest is generated in a specific area of the family, the reader may want to turn to some of the readings suggested in the selected bibliographies. It is obvious, but should not be left unstated, that this book is dependent upon the works of others.

R.R.B.

CONTENTS

Studies in

MARRIAGE AND THE FAMILY

ENGAGEMENT AND MARRIAGE

Ernest W. Burgess and Paul Wallin

Most members of most societies reach a period during their adolescence or in their early adult years when marriage occurs. In every culture, one may have a variety of persons of the opposite sex as possible marital partners, but in no culture is the selection of a specific partner one of random choice. In all cultures, there are some restrictions imposed by society in addition to the restrictions of individual tastes and values. The restrictions placed by society may focus around such variables as being of "proper" age, not being married already, not being related too closely to the selected partner, and so forth. The individual values usually center around the satisfaction of one's ego-needs—in the United States it is of great importance to have one's love object return the love.

In American society, mate selection is a gradual process that starts with dating and moves through the stages of the courtship process. It does not happen to an individual "all of a sudden," but is the culmination of the young person's experiences over a number of

---

Source: Pp. 187–213 from ENGAGEMENT AND MARRIAGE, by Ernest W. Burgess and Paul Wallin (Philadelphia: J. P. Lippincott Company, 1953). Reprinted by permission of Paul Wallin.

years. Influenced by his previous experiences and personal needs, a person reaching the age of marriage starts to concentrate on a particular individual. His values have been pretty well established by the time he reaches the usual age of marriage, and the general type of person he will marry has, within reasonable limits, already been determined.

The experiences leading up to mate selection, and the values involved, combine emotional with rational factors. Anthropological findings show that, whenever people are free to choose their own mates, individual and personal motives come into play. The direction of choice, whether romantic or rational, will vary with different individuals. The young person selecting his own mate today places far greater importance on the personal and emotional factors than did his parents, who grew up in an era of more active parental help in mate selection for the offspring.

During the ten-year period from 1936 to 1946, Burgess and Wallin studied 1,000 engaged and 666 married couples. They gathered data with reference to all the social and personal variables believed to be related to mate selection. The respondents studied do not constitute a random sample of the population, but are biased in the direction of the higher educated and higher social classes. Because the study was completed a number of years ago, the findings may be somewhat dated. However, the primary reason for including this study is that it is the largest sample studied in the most comprehensive way on the subject of mate selection, and it does provide us with a number of insights into mate selection, insights probably as accurate today as they were twenty-five years ago.

CHOOSING A MATE

The expected, approved, and sanctioned precondition to marriage in American society is falling in love. According to our mores love is the only right basis for marriage.

But why does a man or woman fall in love? Many people,

old as well as young, believe there is no answer to this question. They regard falling in love as a unique and mysterious experience. They do not consider it a proper subject for scientific inquiry.

The Burgess-Wallin interviews with young people and a recent study by Anselm Strauss[1] indicate the operation of a number of factors in the choice of a mate. The factors which seem to influence falling in love and mate selection are propinquity, image of an ideal mate, parental image, personality needs, and homogamy. Homogamy means the tendency of like to attract like in falling in love. It is to be distinguished from heterogamy which means attraction of opposites to each other.

Propinquity

There can be no doubt that propinquity, defined as spacial proximity, operates in mate selection. The findings of various studies[2] are in agreement that a far greater number of marriages than could be expected by chance occur among young people who live in proximity, work at the same occupation, attend the same church, and are members of the same recreational groups. But this may only mean that young people, to fall in love and marry, must first meet and become acquainted. To be the sole and decisive factor in mate selection, propinquity requires a situation of isolation of a couple from others. This situation occurs, for example, when a man and woman are shipwrecked on a desert isle. In this case, isolation and the absence of any other social contacts determine their choice. Situations of

[1] Anselm Strauss, *A Study of Three Psychological Factors Affecting Choice of a Mate* (Chicago: University of Chicago Libraries, Ph.D. Thesis, 1945).

[2] *See,* for example, James H. S. Bossard, "Residential Propinquity as a Factor in Marriage Selection," *American Journal of Sociology,* 38, 1932–1933, pp. 219–224; Maurice R. Davie and Ruby Jo Reeves, "Propinquity of Residence Before Marriage," *American Journal of Sociology,* 44, 1938–39, pp. 510–517; Ruby Jo Reeves Kennedy, "Premarital Residential Propinquity and Ethnic Endogamy," *American Journal of Sociology,* 48, 1942–1943, pp. 580–584; Donald M. Marvin, "Occupational Propinquity as a Factor in Marriage Selection," *Journal of the American Medical Association,* 16, 1918–1919, pp. 131–150.

relative social isolation may have a similar outcome. Two Easterners at a dude ranch, the only two Americans in a Rumanian village, two young people in a tourist group of older persons, are cases where the range of selection is so greatly reduced that propinquity alone may lead to love.

In other situations propinquity may be less obvious but quite as effective a factor. The shy and quiet young man who finds it difficult to meet girls may fall in love with his landlady's daughter, with his high school teacher, or with the first girl who shows a sympathetic interest in him. Or the heiress, sheltered from association with youths, may become romantically in love with her music teacher, with her father's chauffeur, or with the lifeguard at the private bathing beach.

These illustrations imply that propinquity operates as a decisive factor in direct proportion to the fewness of social contacts. The greater the number of potential marriage partners in a given situation of propinquity, the less the effect of this factor and the greater the influence of other factors in mate selection, such as image of an ideal mate, parental image, and personality need. Accordingly, except in cases of the absence or scarcity of social contacts, propinquity may be regarded as a limiting rather than as a decisive influence in the choice of mates. We must look to other factors to find out "who mates with whom" and why.

We should not overlook the barriers which make for social distance even when persons are physically near each other. Two young people may be in close physical proximity but may be widely separated socially. Social distance, determined by differences in ethnic groups, social classes, and age groups, usually constitutes an effective barrier to acquaintance and friendship. These cultural influences are frequently internalized in the attitudes of the person and influence the formation of the image of the ideal mate.

Image of Ideal Mate

The term ideal mate implies that a person has a mental picture of the idealized characteristics of the one he wishes to marry. This image, as will be seen later, may be vague and indefinite or clear and distinct. In adolescence the "dream" man or girl is perceived in his physical attributes: physique, beauty of face or form, and in striking psychological traits of courage and daring, charm and poise. Young people name these attributes sometimes in symbolic language:[3]

My ideal was sort of childish—like seeing your Prince Charming riding in on a white horse.

Sometimes these attitudes are stated very concretely:

My preference was for a girl who was blonde, petite, and cute.

My ideal was more or less a physical ideal of how he'd look, and his likes and dislikes, and not his character. I wanted him to be about 6′ 2″, a great big fellow, and have red hair. And I wanted him to be a football star. I wanted him to be very smooth and always know the right time to do things.

A childish ideal—someone good looking and wealthy. I always had an idea of having a huge home, jewels and furs and things. I imagined a man who looked very well in tails and made a good host at a dinner party.

The image of the ideal mate, with its emphasis upon physical attributes, is not, however, always entirely romantic. It usually includes social characteristics which in general emphasize more practical considerations of similarity in race, nationality, religious faith, standards of conduct, socio-economic status, education, political views, and so on. On further association with the opposite sex it generally comes to embrace congeniality in tastes, interests, and ideals, and to stress compatibility in personality traits. The following excerpts illustrate the way in which young people express their desires that certain of these more significant characteristics be found in their future mates:

[3] The case materials cited in this chapter are drawn from the interviews of the Burgess–Wallin and Strauss studies.

Girl. My ideal was mainly a construction of qualities with very little thought about physical characteristics. My fiancé has the outstanding qualities which I had hoped my life mate might have. My ideal acted as a measuring stick, you might say as a standard of value, of worth. I consciously studied my fiancé and if I had found him to be dishonest, cruel, and without ideals I would never have married him. But factors such as religion, common background, character, smoking, drinking, and appearance, set up as standards for my ideal, were very important in my choice. I knew I would not be happy otherwise.

Girl. I superficially divided people into real people and those who just enjoyed good times. My brother's friends were the latter kind. I just couldn't stand people like that. I wanted people I could talk to. And someone who wouldn't care if I was terribly sophisticated or not. And someone who had all the qualities that I'd want—such as being sincere with a girl, being honest, not aggressive, had the drive to get ahead, and conscientious. And he had to be intelligent—someone who thinks and has ideas and philosophizes on things and someone who does enjoy reading and music. And I always realized I wanted someone easy to get along with.

Man. I've always felt that I would like a girl clean in speech, no bad habits, neither smokes nor drinks, good family, good appearance and figure. I've always had as my ideal a church-going girl with clean thoughts. That's why I'd say my fiancée has always been to my mind an ideal girl. To me she typifies everything I had ever wished for in a girl, ever since I've been clear enough to think about it. She typifies purity, attractiveness, understanding, fineness; probably all the qualities that are connected with my ideal.

These quotations indicate that as young people become socially mature they tend to minimize the external and superficial traits stressed by the adolescent group. This growing appreciation of personality and cultural traits marks also the transition from crushes and infatuation to the companionship pattern in the relation of the sexes.

The 173 men and 200 women studied by Strauss named the traits included in their conception of an ideal mate. Half the group were engaged and half were in the first year of marriage. Almost all had had some college education. These traits were classified as physical, cultural, and temperamental. Excluding those not replying (most of whom stated that they did not have or did not know of such traits) nearly every young man and young woman reported one or more physical and one or more cultural traits. These latter included religion, nationality, and education. Only half the women and less than two-fifths of the men mentioned temperamental characteristics such as shyness, excitability, moodiness, and artistic nature.

The image of the ideal mate is often quite explicit and in the forefront of consciousness. Sometimes, however, the image is

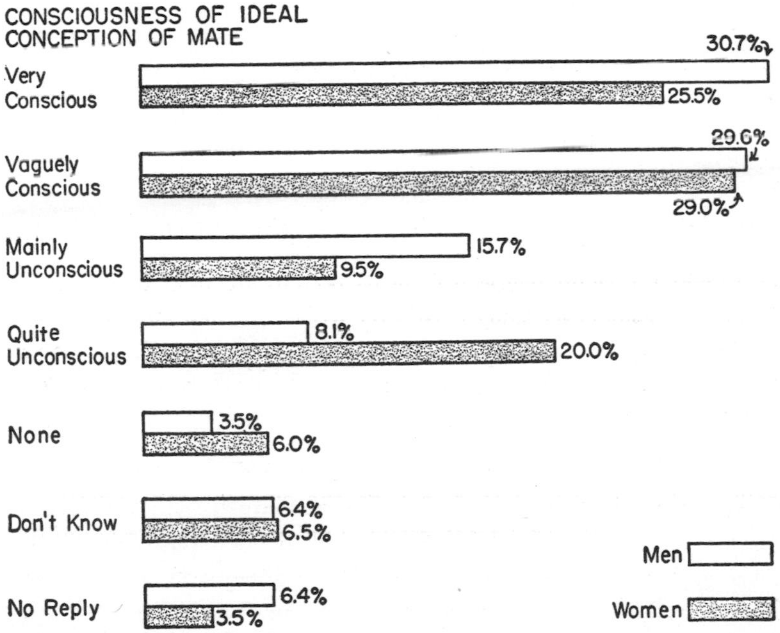

Chart 1: Per cent of men and women reporting different degrees of consciousness of ideal conception of mate in choosing a fiancé(e).

vague or only partly conscious. Chart 1 indicates the degree to which one group of engaged and married young people were conscious or unaware (by their own reports) of a conception of an ideal mate. More than half these young men and women state they were conscious in varying degrees of possessing such an image. It is interesting that a higher proportion of women than of men deny being conscious of this idealized conception.

Even where the person is unconscious of any image which functions to guide the selection of a mate he is more or less aware of those who would be excluded as matrimonial possibilities. Take, for example, a college girl of New England ancestry of the upper middle class, whose Congregational church membership has been inherited for several generations. She will not consider for a husband a lower-middle-class youth who is working his way through a barber college and whose last name is unpronounceably foreign. Her image of a mate, even if not clear-cut, automatically excludes men of a lower social class, of different ethnic stock, and of divergent religious affiliation. In the following case the girl had no concrete dream man, but she admitted having certain standards for selection:

I never had a dream man. I never pictured the kind of a person I wanted to fall in love with. And I never fell in love with movie stars. One thing I wasn't conscious of wanting. I never had a crush on any easy-going fellow. I had to have a he-man. I could never have fallen in love with anyone not Jewish. I had a rather thorough upbringing and I just never thought of going outside my own circle. I wasn't looking for money.

In fact, a chief function of the image of the ideal mate is negative. It eliminates many persons with whom one may be in proximity from any consideration at all as matrimonial possibilities. Strauss found that the young men and women he studied had consciously excluded as potential mates persons with certain characteristics. The attributes leading to exclusion, in terms of the percentages of men and women stating them, were respectively: different race, 49.7, 65.5; different religion, 41.6, 42.5; difference in educational status, 33.5, 40.5; different social background, 27.8, 34.0;

physical defect, 27.2, 26.5; markedly different political views, 28.9, 22.0; different economic status, 23.1, 20.5; not handsome or good-looking, 22.0, 13.5; nonprofessional occupation, 9.8, 16.5; not native American, 11.6, 15.5.[4]

These conscious exclusions are undoubtedly less frequent than unconscious eliminations; young college people, especially, are prone to think of themselves as more tolerant of differences than they actually are.

It is also interesting to note the sex differences in the conscious characterization of those barred from consideration as possible mates. Women differ significantly from men in the emphasis on differences in race. Men, on the other hand, differ significantly from women in their stress on personal beauty.

The original image of the ideal mate is sometimes closely approximated in the fiancé. The girl in the following case found the particular combination of characteristics she most desired:

I wanted him to be smooth, you know—be able to fit into any situation. Oh, he's got to be tall. And must have brown eyes—I'd feel just gypped if he didn't have brown eyes. And oh, I wanted a good figure, not skinny or fat you know. And a good dancer—not flashy, but a good sense of rhythm, not like a businessman's pace you know—you can go to the Panther room and have a good time. I'd like for him to know how to dress too—look nice. Oh I left out the most important thing!—I wanted him to be real smart. Real smart: get good grades. Be good in things like chemistry and mathematics. And yet know references to things like the classics and in English—well just be real educated; I guess that goes along with being smooth. And know classical music, you know, hear just a piece of it and know who wrote it and what it is, and their life history. And know where to take you, where's a good place to eat and where to dance, really can know a good show, and when he comes over he has a plan that's better than I can think of. Oh yes, and a guy

[4] *Op. cit. See also* two other studies of college students who list characteristics that cause them to exclude certain persons as potential mates, *see* R. E. Baber, *Marriage and the Family* (New York: McGraw-Hill Book Co.), p. 149, and J. T. and Mary S. Landis, *Building a Successful Marriage* (New York: Prentice-Hall, 1948), p. 85.

that wasn't interested in any other girl than me. Because I don't want to be jealous. That we can go to parties and he can be real nice to girl friends and sorority sisters. And everybody knows he was with me and not get drunk and start kissing all the girls. That's another thing, I don't like a man to get drunk. And let's see. I guess to sum it all, just smooth acting and looking right, at the right time.

Bill fits pretty close. He doesn't have real dark hair, you know, like Cary Grant. He dresses all right. He came here on a scholarship and knows all the classics. And played trumpet in the band so he knows all the classical music. Well, I think he's a real intellectual. And he'll go to dances at his fraternity and know lots of the girls and kid around with them and dance and never try to show me by flirting with any of the girls. He kinda knows where to go and what mood I'm in. And he's not a flashy dancer, but he's a good dancer. And he has real dark-brown eyes.

Sometimes the real mate is markedly different, particularly in physical characteristics:

I just had insignificant little ideas that I thought important. But when you don't even put in character, and you just put in blond hair, that just doesn't mean very much.

In the following case the girl changed her expectations to meet the personal characteristics of her fiancé:

The man I had pictured wasn't a human being; or if he was, he was a too perfect human being. I've met people like that since then and I wouldn't look at them twice. They don't have any minds of their own—they do just what is considered proper. The more Lloyd had broken down this image the more I cared for him—because that was when I found the real person inside.

Strauss asked his group of engaged and married couples to comment on the question: "How important do you feel the 'ideal' was in picking your fiancé(e)?" His data indicate that only 19 per cent of the men and 26 per cent of the women reported that the image of the ideal mate was unimportant. Two-thirds of the men and about the same proportion of the women believed it was important or at least of some importance.

When the person with whom one falls in love diverges markedly from the idealized expectation, other factors to be discussed later prove to be more significant. A chief effect, then, of the image of an ideal mate seems to be to exclude those who do not measure up to it. This is particularly so when the person is not too conscious of it. In a large proportion of cases, however, it acts as a positive selective factor. The young man marries the girl who corresponds with the glamorous picture in his imagination or the young woman chooses her blond hero with the sky-blue eyes and the glint of gold in his hair.

Particularly where physical characteristics determine the selection, the union is likely to be one of romantic infatuation with love at first sight. Frequently, in our society, attachments based on the idealization of certain physical attributes tend to disintegrate unless they are supported by more binding factors in mate selection. This is borne out by an interesting finding of Strauss' study: [5]

> Rivals and fiancés are more or less alike with regard to resembling the physical ideal. On the other hand fiancés resemble the personality ideal a good deal more closely than do rivals. This suggests the relative unimportance of the physical ideal for marital choice as compared with the important association of mate and personality ideal.

This finding strongly suggests that the physical characteristics of the ideal mate function in the initial selection in courtship, but that the idealized personality traits have a more significant role in the final selection of a life partner.

The question remains as to what determines the rise and development of a particular image of the ideal mate. Is it largely cultural in origin, deriving from the physical and psychological characteristics that are approved by adolescents and youth in our society, such as those presented by the motion picture? Or does it emerge from individual differences in experience in the affectional relationships with one's parents in childhood?

Probably both factors, the cultural and the psychogenic,

[5] *Op. cit.*, pp. 47–48.

operate. Perhaps at first and on the more superficial level of preliminary association the cultural factor is more important, as in romantic affairs; and later the psychological factors of parental image and personality needs become more significant, particularly in companionship unions. We turn, therefore, to a consideration of these two factors in mate selection.

Parental Image

The theory that parental image is a factor in mate selection assumes that a person tends to fall in love and to marry someone with the personality characteristics of the parent of the opposite sex, provided that the affectional relationship with the parent had been satisfying to him as a child. Typically, the boy feels attracted to a girl who resembles his mother, and the girl to a young man who is like her father.

The interviews with engaged couples revealed certain interesting differences in the actual effect of parental image upon mate selection. These will be discussed in terms of (1) the nature of parental image, (2) patterns of parental image, and (3) the role of parental image in mate selection.

NATURE OF PARENTAL IMAGE: The manifestations of parental image may be divided into (*a*) the physical resemblance of the fiancé(e) to father or to mother, (*b*) the correspondence of their temperamental and other personality traits, (*c*) the similarity of the affectional and emotional relationship between the loved one and the parent of the opposite or sometimes of the same sex.

Cases will be presented showing these three kinds of resemblance. At this point, therefore, only a few brief clarifying comments are offered.

Typical physical resemblances between the fiancé(e) and parent were in physique, posture, carriage, physiognomy, and facial expression. Similarities in temperament and other personality traits differed widely from case to case. Occasionally nearly all the traits of the mother and of the fiancée were reported by the young man to be identical. More often a few characteristics in his mother which he had felt important to him had been duplicated in his girl. Sometimes only one or two of the most significant traits in his mother appeared in his reports of his fiancée. Some of the more discerning young people decided upon reflection that the resemblances in physical appearance and personality were not as important to them as the affectional relation to their mates which was similar to the one sustained with a given parent, generally of the opposite sex, in childhood.

Some engaged persons specify resemblance between the parent and the love object in a particular response relation such as attentiveness, display of affection, sympathy, understanding, stimulation, and encouragement. Other young people stress the similarity in a rather more generalized relationship such as feelings of rapport, relaxation, and ease. This sense of feeling "at home" with their affianced, which was felt with the parent, they place in contrast to their reactions of tenseness or being ill-at-ease in earlier pair relationships.

PATTERNS OF PARENTAL IMAGE: Parental images, as reported by engaged persons, fall into certain patterns. The first and most usual is where the loved one resembles the parent of the opposite sex. Quite often this is found in both members of an engaged couple. In the following case the girl resembles the young man's mother, not only in physical and personality traits but also in the nature of her affectional and emotional relationship to him:

> Lucy's resemblance to my mother struck me. I think it was her walk and her smile. She had a lot of ambition. Both of them are ambitious. Mother has tried to make corrections in Dad. The young lady has the same tendency. They are not physically alike except that they walk the same way. They are the same height. My mother is rather lean, while Lucy is inclined to chubbiness. My mother is a dark blonde, and my fiancée is a brunette.

The girl on the other hand describes the young man as a duplicate of her father in physical appearance and personality traits:

There is a physical resemblance between Carl and my father. My father now is heavy, but when he was young, they were almost the same size. They might have been dead ringers for one another. They have blue eyes, sandy hair; undecided blonde, I call it. They have long fingers. They are both very patient and unselfish. Neither one of them gets angry very suddenly or bears any grudges. They are both stubborn to a certain extent. They have minds of their own. They are reserved. They both have the same respect for women. Mother and I have often remarked about their resemblance. Others have, too.

A second pattern, reported less frequently by engaged couples, might be called the "reverse" parental image. It is represented by cases where the parent image reproduced by the mate is not that of the parent of the opposite sex, but of the same sex:

I would never want to marry anyone like my father—fond as I am of him I couldn't stand being married to someone like him. I'm a little too much like him. My father came from a family which spoiled him and he had a very wonderful mother and was sort of tied to her apron strings. And Ed isn't. So that I don't have the competition with Ed's family that my mother is constantly faced with. Both Mother and Ed have open personalities—both are well liked and are good company. People will confide in Mother and also in Ed. I think they're very much alike in the way they look at people. Mother's much more easy in what she thinks of people than my father.

A third pattern, not as frequent as others among engaged couples, is that of the negative parental image. In this pattern the person reports being attracted to someone the direct opposite of the parent in one or more personality characteristics. One girl states that she was attracted to her fiancé by his trait of dominating, which she desired in a husband because she disliked the passive role played by her father in his marriage:

One thing I didn't like about my father was that he was too passive. I mean he agreed too much. My mother made all the plans, and although they worked out perfectly satisfactorily, I don't like that. I mean I don't like that for myself. One thing I always wanted was not to be the boss—I mean I always wanted someone who would stand up for his own rights.

That was one thing wrong with those other boys. They were so "in love" that everything I said was all right with them. And I wanted someone, I guess, who was a little stronger than that. At one time I thought Joey looked a little like a gangster. Other people don't think so, but you know what I mean. I think that's kind of significant now that I think of it. Because a gangster to me—well, a gangster has the connotation of being a real man. Wait—maybe it's that he hasn't got a weak-looking face—it has a certain strength—I think that comes closer to it.

A fourth and quite frequent pattern in mate selection is a combination of those traits of both parents which had a positive response value in the childhood relation. Often the trait appreciated in the parent of the same sex is the reverse of a characteristic greatly disliked in the other parent. This is true in the case of Nancy, who was irritated by her father's disagreeable temperament. She became engaged to George, who resembled her father in his other outstanding personality traits but her mother in temperament:

I'd say George was more like my father than my mother. Neither of them will let things slide—both are very punctual, very precise—that's probably because of their training. They both know what they want and they're out to get it. And I think they are both rather shrewd businessmen. Their personalities are very much the same. They're both great kidders and jokers. I'd say their personalities were very similar. But their temperaments are different—very different. George is like my father in personality and my mother in temperament. He's built very similar to my father. He's a little shorter, but he's heavy, like my father. And they're both broad-shouldered, large hands and feet. Mother has a very good disposition and shows it to everyone. She and George are two of the kindest people I've ever seen in my life. Neither would ever hurt anyone. George never forgets anything and neither does my mother. They never forget birthdays or Christmas or the little things. That's the primary attraction—because George is so very thoughtful and he seems to think more of me than most of the boys.

Besides these four patterns of parental image, certain "surrogate" or substitute images are occasionally found. Where a person's response relation in childhood was not significant with either parent, there may be a surrogate image of a grandparent, an older brother or sister, an uncle or an aunt, or a friendly and admired adult outside the family. The parental substitute, as pointed out by Strauss, functions in accordance with the theory of the parental image.[6]

THE ROLE OF PARENTAL IMAGE IN MATE SELECTION: Certain points should be made on the way in which parental image appears to influence mate selection. These are exemplified in the extracts just quoted and in other cases interviewed. First, parental image often seems to be an effective factor in mate selection. It is not primarily merely a limiting factor, as is generally the case with propinquity and image of the ideal mate. Second, it is not usually a superficial factor, at least with college young people, like the adolescent's picture of an ideal mate; occasionally it is, however, as when a youth is attracted to a girl because of her physical resemblance to his mother. Generally, at least with persons at the college level, the paternal image seems to function more effectively in terms of personality traits and of specific affectional and response resemblances rather than of physical likeness.

Third, the resemblance between the parent and the loved one is seldom perceived by engaged persons. Sometimes they say that others note similarities which they do not see. One girl states, "People say that Dad and Joe resemble each other physically, but I've never quite seen it." In fact, many of the interviewed couples did not become aware of a similarity until it was brought out, often to their great surprise, by their answers to questions in the interview.

Fourth, the operation of the parental image in mate selection is, as yet, not too fully understood. In analyzing the cases, certain patterns of selection emerge. These have already been identified as the attraction of a person for someone (1) with the characteristics of the parent of the opposite sex, (2) with the traits of the parent of the same sex, (3) with attributes which are the direct opposite of a parent, (4) with characteristics combining those of both parents, and (5) with traits of the surrogate (or substitute) of the parent,

[6] *See* Anselm Strauss, *op. cit.*, pp. 85, 90.

such as grandparent, older brother, older sister, other relative, or other adult.

The question of greatest interest is why a person follows one pattern and not another. Certain answers may be tentatively offered. One explanation appears applicable to the majority of cases. It is that the person tends to fall in love with someone who resembles the parent or parent surrogate with whom he was affectionately closest as a child. A secondary explanation seems to cover a much smaller proportion of cases. If there has been an unsatisfactory relation with one parent (typically of the other sex), the person is attracted to an individual with directly opposite characteristics. These are cases of the negative parental image.

There is some evidence that the person in selecting a mate chooses one that will continue or reproduce, as nearly as possible, the total home atmosphere. Often, as in the last case reported, the person seems to find a mate possessing the chief characteristics admired in both parents, but without a trait disliked in one of them.

A factor even more powerful in mate selection than the parental image is that of personality need. The two factors are undoubtedly closely related. The emotional interaction of the person in childhood with his parents is probably of great significance in determining his personality need. Moreover, personality need in some cases—as explained below—may be the explanation of the operation of parental image in mate selection.

Personality Need

By the term *personality need,* as used in this chapter, is meant the desire for those satisfactions which are obtained through intimate association with other persons. The family provides human relationships especially significant for the satisfaction of the basic needs of the person. Among the needs which men and women hope to satisfy in marriage are love and affection, confidence, sympathy, understanding, dependence, encouragement, intimate appreciation, and emotional security.

These needs are sometimes eminently satisfied in relations

with one or both parents. Consequently, if one finds a mate with these parental personality characteristics, these needs will continue to be satisfied.

The personality needs which engaged couples reveal explicitly or implicitly may be stated as follows: (1) general versus specific needs, (2) many needs as compared with only a few, one, or none at all, (3) mutual satisfaction of needs in contrast to lack of satisfaction by one or both, and (4) the degree of satisfaction of major personality needs.

GENERAL VERSUS SPECIFIC NEEDS: Engaged persons may express their need for each other in specific or in general terms. In the following case the girl finds that the young man satisfies needs for understanding, encouragement, and approval:

Harlowe is an understanding person, quite unselfish; the kind of person I had never known before, the kind I could freely talk with on any subject and not feel inhibited. I do need quite a good deal of encouragement and approval. I like to be told I'm doing right. He gives me encouragement. I get discouraged rather easily and he gets me out of it. Harlowe gets discouraged a little but not as much as I by any means. He needs sympathy and encouragement too. I don't feel that he needs it as much as I.

Harlowe mentions specific needs as companionship, common interests, similarity of tastes, temperamental congeniality, the art of being a good listener, and encouragement.

She has a combination of all the things I would ask for. We were friends before we cared at all about each other. She can enter into almost any activity that happens to come along. We have done lots of things together and find we have similar tastes in everything. We are rather alike in temperament, except that she is more steady. When we first started going together she filled the need of having a good listener. She does not discourage or disparage one's efforts. On the other hand, she encourages them. I don't think you could say I have any full-fledged need for sympathy or understanding. We seem to fulfill each other's requirements on that score.

The emotional interdependence of the couple may not be in terms of either general or specific personality needs. Instead, it may be a generalized feeling of ease, relaxation, and happiness in the association:

Will makes me feel very happy. I always feel comfortable, at ease, with him. With some boys I feel just a little uneasy—I wonder what they're thinking of—I never quite know. I always have a good time with Will and if such goes on it sounds like an idyllic arrangement. I know he'd never do anything knowingly to make me unhappy, and I know I'd never do anything knowingly to make him unhappy. And I'm sure of his feelings for me which makes it easier for me because I have a fear of letting myself go and not know whether they're reciprocated or not.

MANY NEEDS IN CONTRAST WITH A FEW, ONE, OR NONE: Some persons are especially dependent on a mate for satisfaction of a wide range of personality needs. A few claim to be emotionally independent and self-sufficient. One girl lists many needs which her fiancé meets:

Lawrence gives me what I want—he remembers little things—I think little things are important. He remembers birthdays. We have a lot in common, we like to do things together. That's something my mother and father don't have—that's always amazed me. It will be a sort of give-and-take relationship. Lawrence doesn't tend to dominate me and tell me what to do—and that satisfies me, I need that. And I can ask for advice and get it, but he doesn't insist on his way being the only way. We like to do pretty much the same things. We like sports that we can do together, and we like to dance. And I just like being together with him, which was something I could never do with any other boy; we always had to be doing something, and I got tired. There's a physical satisfaction too—we're compatible. He isn't too pressing that way—neither am I—so there's a nice balance. I like someone I can talk over things and sort of come back to, like discussing the day's work. I like someone I feel loves me too; I feel that very strongly. I don't want criticism, but someone who understands my moods.

Other couples report only a few needs. Oscar J., for example, has the need for encouragement to an unusually high degree, while his fiancée, Irene L., feels the need of his sympathy, encouragement, and stabilizing influence:

I seem to be content with her, and I'm dissatisfied when I'm away from her. She encourages me. I don't know whether she just agrees with me or what, but when I make plans with her they seem more logical or sensible. I tell her when I'm disgusted or discouraged with my work, and she listens and makes me feel better. I've always said I was self-sufficient, but more and more I feel the need for her. I've always said that even though I love her, if she were to leave me I could go on, but as time goes on I feel less sure of that. I think my personality is of such a nature that it fits in very well with hers. She says she feels very calm and satisfied when she's with me or in my arms. Some of her relatives used to tell me that she was flighty and needed a balance wheel, and after we'd been going together a while she told me I was her balance wheel.

I seem to be calmer with him. He has acted as a balance wheel for me. I think I need sympathy and encouragement. Even if he's only telling me what I already know, I like to hear it.

In a very few cases one or both state that they are emotionally independent. For example, John A. and Polly T. claim they are self-sufficient, and she adds that even if a man wished sympathy she would not grant it:

I don't think I need encouragement. I have enough confidence in myself. I feel that Polly can take responsibility the same way that I can.

I think I am self-sufficient. Jack has never had occasion to give me sympathy and encouragement. I think at times he needs encouragement. I don't believe in sympathizing; especially with men. They require too much sympathy. They are just pampered.

MUTUAL SATISFACTION OF NEEDS: Engaged couples may report needs which are or are not reciprocally satisfied. An interesting example of reciprocal satisfaction is where both the man and the woman have ups and downs in moods but are able to help each other, as in the following case:

Doris gets blue moods now and then and I try to pick her up. She does the same for me when I get mine. I don't have them as often as I used to.

Sometimes I can't seem to get at him. He seems to have a load on his chest and does not try to get it off. He does not do a lot of complaining. He is too likely to be too shut-up. Sometimes sympathy helps. Once in a while I get depressed and pull myself together and get out of it. I'm not chronically depressed. Occasionally he helps; other times I get out of it myself.

Sometimes only one member of a couple has a need which the other meets. In the following case the girl gives encouragement to the man but is herself quite self-sufficient:

I do need encouragement and Janette gives it to me. Last year when things looked pretty bad and I didn't know where I was heading she came forward and discussed it and she would get me in a different frame of mind. I don't think she needs sympathy and encouragement. I think she is quite self-sufficient.

I find Elmer a very good companion. On the whole we seem to have a common understanding of each other. I think I'm self-sufficient. I do get depressed. I don't think anyone gets me out of it. He needs sympathy and encouragement. I try to give it to him. He is rather self-sufficient.

DEGREE OF SATISFACTION OF MAJOR PERSONALITY NEEDS: In only a small minority of cases does an engaged person find that all his major personality needs are satisfied by his affianced. Strauss [7] calculated the extent to which the major personality needs are fulfilled by one's fiancé(e). He asked his engaged and married subjects to indicate their major personality needs by underlining them in a list of 26 items presented as follows:

I have a need for someone
to stimulate my ambition,
to confide in,
who appreciates what I want to achieve,

[7] *Op. cit.*, p. 166.

who will stand back of me whatever difficulty I'm in,
who admires my ability,
who makes me feel I count for something,
who gives me self-confidence in my relations with people,
who doesn't criticize me for failings and weaknesses,
etc.

Later he asked his subjects to check the degree to which the major needs they had reported were fulfilled by the fiancé(e), i.e., "very much," "considerably," "a little," "not at all," "opposite."[8] Strauss then computed the percentage of the total number of major needs of each subject which were "very much" satisfied by the fiancé(e). For example, a person indicating four needs and checking two of them as fulfilled "very much" would be classified as having 50 per cent of his needs met by the fiancé(e).

For the majority of engaged and married persons studied by Strauss there is more or less discrepancy between their expressed major personality needs and the degree to which these are "very much" filled by their mates. This is clearly shown by an examination of Chart 2.

Only 18 per cent of the men and women report that all their major personality needs are satisfied in the relationship with their fiancé(e)s or spouses. An additional 12 per cent of the men and 24 per cent of the women state that at least four-fifths, but not all of their needs, are fulfilled. On the other hand, 29 per cent of the males and 18 per cent of the females report that less than two-fifths of their needs are being satisfied in their relation.

The conclusion to be drawn is that a high proportion of persons fail to find the satisfaction of their chief personality needs in their relation with their mates. Yet the fulfillment of personality needs appears to be of primary importance in mate selection. The explanation seems to be that the majority of individuals strike a compromise in securing the satisfaction of some or even most personality needs, but not all of them.

The purpose of the foregoing discussion is to throw light

[8] *Ibid.*, p. 166.

upon the role of personality needs in mate selection. For this reason the personality needs of the person were taken as they were reported in the engagement period. It is, therefore, not essential to explain their origin and development. It is sufficient to ask only three questions: "What are the personality needs of an individual in the area of intimate relations?" "Do these personality needs play a part in the selection of a mate?" "Are these personality needs being satisfied in the relationship?"

Homogamy

More than 100 studies have been made of a factor which investigators have thought to be of great importance in mate selection. This

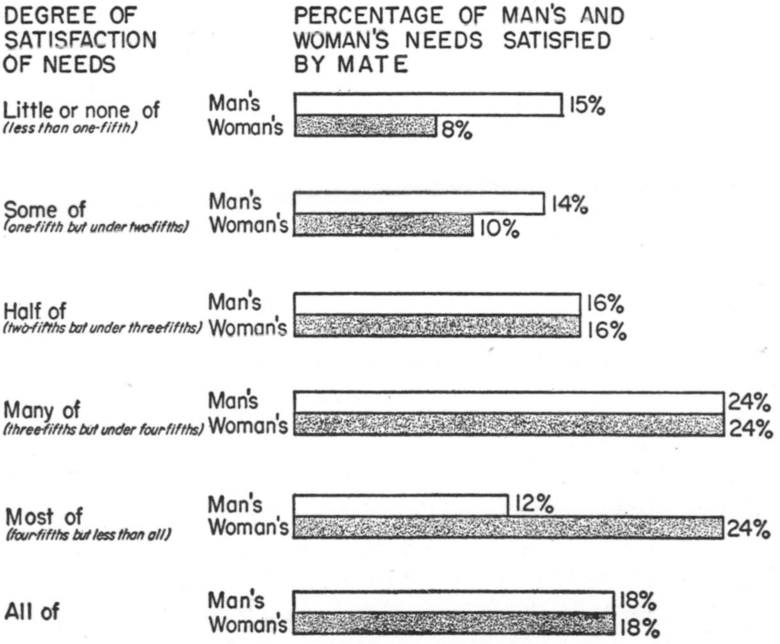

Chart 2: Percentage of major personality needs satisfied by mate as reported by 120 men and women in the study by Strauss.

factor is homogamy, which literally means the marriage of persons of like characteristics. It is the opposite of heterogamy, which signifies the union of people of different traits.

Popular opinion appears almost evenly divided between those who think that "like mates with like" and those who believe that "opposites attract."

All previous studies[9] with an adequate number of cases arrive at the conclusion that in every trait which varies from chance expectation the tendency is for "like to mate with like." This unanimity of findings seemed to clinch the case for homogamy as an important factor in mate selection. All but one, however, of these earlier studies were of married couples and were open to the criticism that marriage might have created similarities or accentuated them.

In the study of 1000 engaged couples a considerable amount of social, psychological, and physical data were obtained on both the young man and his fiancée. This provided a large body of information about characteristics of a couple whose likeness or unlikeness on these characteristics could not be attributed to their association during married life.

The findings from the study of engaged couples are in general agreement with previous studies of married couples. On no trait was there a preponderance of heterogamous unions over chance. Whenever there was a statistically significant difference it was in the direction that "like mates with like."

Homogamy was studied in 88 traits of the engaged young people. Very few of the 51 social characteristics had been investigated in the studies of homogamy with married couples. Findings were also secured on 5 physical and 31 personality characteristics.

[9] Bibliographies on studies of homogamy are to be found in C. A. Anderson, "The Sociological Approach to the Study of Assortative Mating," *International Congress for Studies Regarding Population Problems* 8, 1932, pp. 600–634, and Helen M. Richardson, "Studies of Mental Resemblances between Husbands and Wives and between Friends," *Psychological Bulletin*, 36, 1939, pp. 104–120.

Table 1: Similarity of Members of Engaged Couples on Social Characteristics

	Ratio of Actual to Expected Similarity *
RELIGIOUS AFFILIATION AND BEHAVIOR	
Religious affiliation (Catholic, Protestant, Jewish, none)	2.14
Church attendance	1.69
Sunday-school attendance (stopped before age of 11, at 11–18, at 19 or over)	1.42
Church membership	1.43
FAMILY BACKGROUNDS	
Place lived in childhood (large city, small city, suburb, town, village)	1.49
Nativity of parents (both native-born, one foreign-born, both foreign-born)	1.48
Education (graduate and professional, college, high school or less)	1.37
Present income of parents (under $2,000, $2,000–$4,999, $5,000 and over)	1.34
Social status of parents (leading family, upper class, middle class, lower class)	1.28
Living at present (with parents, relatives, friends, private family, other)	1.25
COURTSHIP BEHAVIOR	
Age began keeping company	1.55
Persons gone with steady besides fiancé(e)	1.27

* It is important to note that of the 51 social traits of engaged couples investigated, only four failed to show a statistically significant preponderance in favor of homogamous unions over those that would have occurred in matching by chance. In Tables 1, 2, 3 the possibilities that the differences between the actual and the expected percentages of similarities of couples could have occurred by chance are less than one out of a hundred.

Table 1: Similarity of Members of Engaged Couples on Social Characteristics (continued)

	Ratio of Actual to Expected Similarity
Discussed engagement (with no one, one, two, three or more persons)	1.25
Previously engaged	1.10
CONCEPTIONS OF MARRIAGE	
Should fiancée work after marriage (no; yes, if necessary; yes, desirable)	1.64
Number of children desired (three or more, one or two, none)	1.42
Attitude toward having children (very much desire, mildly desire, object)	1.31
When spouse ceases to be in love (divorce, separate, continue together)	1.28
Object to fiancé(e) having dates during engagement (yes, no, no issue)	1.26
Head of family (husband, wife, neither)	1.25
Prefer apartment to house (apartment, house, undecided)	1.19
Romantic marriages more successful (yes, no, uncertain)	1.19
Negative factors in conceptions of marriage (none, one, two or more)	1.18
Wife keep own name after marriage (yes, no, other or no reply)	1.19
Divorce justifiable if no unfaithfulness (yes, no, uncertain)	1.15
Present sex knowledge adequate for marriage (yes, no, doubtful)	1.15
Ever marry if not in love (yes, no, uncertain)	1.09
Divorce justifiable (yes, uncertain, no)	1.06
Object to fiancé(e)'s going out with opposite sex (yes, no, other or no reply)	1.06
Positive factors in conceptions of marriage (none or one, two, three or more)	1.07

	Ratio of Actual to Expected Similarity
First sex information (wholesome, partly wholesome, unwholesome)	1.08
SOCIAL PARTICIPATION	
Drinking habits (never, rarely, occasionally or often)	1.81
Smoking habits (does not smoke, will stop if other objects, will not stop)	1.38
Prefer play or dance (play, dance, don't know)	1.31
Leisure-time preferences (stay at home, on go most of time, on go all the time)	1.29
Object if fiancé(e) smokes (no, yes, no answer)	1.12
Friends of opposite sex (none, one to seven, eight or more)	1.10
Organizations regularly attended (none, one or two, three or more)	1.09
Offices in organizations belong to now (none, one, two or more)	1.09
Offices in organizations belonged to in past (none, one, two or more)	1.08
Friends of same sex (none, one to seven, eight or more)	1.07
Considered indifferent to the opposite sex (yes, no, don't know)	1.06
FAMILY RELATIONSHIPS	
Attitude toward father at present (hostile, mildly attached, considerable and strong attachment)	1.11
Attitude to sibling (no sibling, no attachment, attachment to one or more)	1.15
Attitude toward father when a child (hostile, mildly attached, considerable and strong attachment)	1.09
Rating of parents' marriage (very happy, happy, average, unhappy)	1.14
Sex of siblings (only child, female, male, male and female)	1.11

HOMOGAMY IN SOCIAL CHARACTERISTICS: Table 1 shows the degree to which 1000 engaged men and women resembled each other in social characteristics as compared with matings by pure chance.

This comparison is expressed in terms of the ratio of the actual resemblance to expected similarity. The way this ratio is calculated may be concretely illustrated. Everyone knows, for example, that a high proportion of engagements and marriages are of couples of the same as compared with those of different faiths. Usually Catholics mate with Catholics, Jews with Jews, and Protestants with Protestants. But there are also many unions of those with mixed faiths. It is, therefore, interesting to figure the ratio of the actual marrying of "like with like" faith to that which would occur by pure chance. If the 1000 men and the 1000 women in the Burgess-Wallin study had been mated by chance 37.1 per cent would be of the same religious affiliation. Instead of this theoretical expectation, actually those with the same religious affiliation (both Catholic, Jewish, Protestant, and none) are of 79.4 per cent of the couples. The ratio then, of the actual to the similarity expected by chance, is 79.4 per cent divided by 37.1 per cent, or 2.14. By obtaining this ratio it can be definitely stated that engaged couples of this particular study resemble each other in religious affiliation more than twice as often as the theoretical outcome calculated on the basis of mating by pure chance.

An examination of the findings presented in Table 1 shows that, generally, the degree of homogamy is much less than 2.00. It falls as low as 1.06 on belief in justifiability of divorce, objection to fiancé(e) going out with the opposite sex, and considered indifferent to the opposite sex.

The 47 characteristics are classified in six groups. By inspection it will be noted that homogamy is highest in religious affiliation and behavior, then diminishes in ratio of the actual to the expected similarity of the engaged persons according to family backgrounds, courtship behavior, conceptions of marriage, social participation, and reaches its lowest point in family relationships.

A scrutiny of this table also reveals that the variations within five of the six groups of social characteristics are greater than the actual differences between them. For example, traits on which the ratio of actual to expected similarity is about 1.50 or higher appear in five of the groups. These characteristics, in the order in which they appear in Table 1, are religious affiliation (2.14), church attendance (1.69), place lived in childhood (1.49), nativity of parents (1.48), age began keeping company (1.55), agreement on fiancée working after marriage (1.64), and drinking habits (1.81). Also, the degree of homogamy in all the groups except the first two (religious affiliation and behavior) falls as low as 1.06 to 1.11 on one or more social traits.

PHYSICAL CHARACTERISTICS: In five out of six physical characteristics the ratio of actual to expected similarity is greater than chance expectation as shown by Table 2. There is a tendency for tall men and

Table 2: Similarity of Members of Engaged Couples in Physical Characteristics

Characteristic	*Ratio of Actual to Expected Similarity*
Weight in relation to height (above normal, normal, below normal)	1.08
Present state of health (very healthy, healthy, average, poor)	1.17
Complexion (blonde, brunette, in-between)	1.09
Physical appearance of self (very good, fairly good, plain looking)	1.20
Physical appearance of fiancé(e) (very good, good, fair, plain looking)	1.16

women and short men and women to become engaged more than would occur in any random mating. The same principle of like attracting like holds with reference to state of health and physical appearance (both as reported by self and by fiancé(e)).

In only one physical characteristic, that of complexion, was no statistically reliable difference found. Blonds attract blondes, and brunets become engaged to brunettes in about the same proportion as if they were matched by chance.

PERSONALITY CHARACTERISTICS: Of the 42 personality traits studied, 14 showed a greater than chance expectation for homogamous union of engaged couples. As will be seen in Table 3 the differences in the

Table 3: Similarity of Members of Engaged Couples in Personality Characteristics as Indicated by Replies to Thurstone's Neurotic Inventory

Personality Item	*Ratio of Actual to Expected Similarity* *
Neurotic Score	1.13
Do you daydream frequently? **	1.17
Are you frequently burdened by a sense of remorse?	1.10
Are you sometimes the leader at social affairs?	1.11
Does some particular useless thought keep coming into your mind to bother you?	1.05
Do you usually feel that you are well-dressed and make a good appearance?	1.04
Are you touchy on various subjects?	1.14
Do you feel that you must do a thing over several times before you leave it?	1.10
Are your feelings easily hurt?	1.13
Do you often experience periods of loneliness?	1.10
Do ideas often run through your head so you cannot sleep?	1.09
Do your interests change quickly?	1.07
Do you often feel just miserable?	1.06
When you were in school did you hesitate to volunteer in a class recitation?	1.04
Do you get stage fright?	1.10

* The probability that the differences in this table between the actual and expected percentages of similar responses are chance differences is .01 or less.
** All questions could be answered "yes," "no," or "?."

ratio between theoretical expectation of mating of like with like and actual outcome are much smaller for personality than for social characteristics.

But the tendency for persons with neurotic symptoms to be engaged to others like themselves is evident. Correspondingly, nonneurotics unite in engagement with nonneurotics.

The self-ratings by engaged persons indicate homogamy in the degree of day dreaming, loneliness, feelings easily hurt, touchiness, etc. For example, those who characterize themselves as having "feelings easily hurt" or as "being touchy on various subjects" will tend, more than would be expected by chance, to become engaged to those who admit possessing this same trait.

HOMOGAMY OR ASSOCIATION: Of the characteristics studied 47 of 51 social traits, 5 of 6 physical attributes, and 14 of 31 personality self-ratings showed statistically significant differences in the direction of homogamy. No trait showed a preponderance over a chance matching of the couples in favor of the unions in engagement of persons who differ from each other in any characteristic.

The evidence seems to be completely convincing that homogamy is a factor of central importance in mate selection. On a wide range of characteristics, social, physical, and psychological, resemblances among the members of engaged couples predominate over differences. The objection cannot be raised that these resemblances are due to years of association in marriage.

The question should be raised, however, as to what extent the excess of actual matings over chance on the different groups of characteristics considered are due to homogamy rather than to the interaction of the couple in the engagement period. Certainly some of them are clearly not affected by the association of the couple. These are similarities in family cultural backgrounds, courtship behavior, family relationships, and physical characteristics.

The other groups of characteristics may be more or less influenced by the interaction of the engaged couple. For example, religious affiliation may be altered by one member of the couple changing to the other's faith and similarly, church membership and attendance, and even Sunday school attendance, may be affected. But granting even a considerable influence of one member of the couple upon the other, it is hardly sufficient to account for the marked excess of actual over chance expectation of like marrying like. In general, resemblances by religious affiliation and behavior precede rather than follow the association of the couple.

In all the questions dealing with concepts of marriages, with the exception of the wholesomeness of first sex instruction, the association of the couple may account for the resemblances between their answers. There is no way to differentiate between the concepts held by the couple before and after their acquaintance. The only way to determine the relative influence of homogamy and association would be to make a study of concepts of marriage before and after the meeting of the engaged couple. The change in the concepts would reflect the effect of association. The ideas about marriage held by each previous to their acquaintance would be the valid basis for determining the influence of homogamy in mate selection. Provisionally, the middle-of-the-road position may be taken that the similarities in concepts of marriage tend to bring young people together and then to be intensified by their association.

Of the eleven items in social participation, four appear to be almost entirely independent of the association of the engaged couple (number of friends of the same or of the opposite sex, indifferent to the opposite sex, and number of offices held in organizations belonged to in the past). Two that are probably not affected to any great degree by association are number of organizations they regularly attend, and number of offices held in organizations to which they now belong. The others may be somewhat affected by association—leisure-time preferences, prefer play or dance, drinking habits, smoking habits and objection to smoking. The major factor accounting for the similarity of couple members in their leisure-time preferences is probably individual experiences before the couple met, but certainly the possibility of the effect of association cannot be ruled out and the extent of it can only be ascertained by further research.

The likeness in physical characteristics of an engaged man and his fiancée can hardly be attributed to association. Clearly, similarities in height, weight, and physical appearance cannot be the result of association.

Personality characteristics of the couple would also appear to be relatively independent of the association of the young people. In general, tendencies to be "introspective," "stubborn," "selfish," or "moody" and their opposites would seem to be well established before the couple met. The findings that there is a greater tendency for nonneurotics and for neurotics to mate with their kind rather than with others may in part be due to association to the extent that any stress or strain in the relation would affect both members of the couple.

In summary, the conclusion seems valid that association does not account for the finding of the tendency of like to marry like. In five of the eight groups of items—courtship behavior, family backgrounds, physical traits, personality characteristics, and family relationships—the influence of association can be ruled out.

In the remaining groups of items, it is possible but not probable that the similarity of the two engaged persons resulted from their association.

THE ROLE OF HOMOGAMY IN MATE SELECTION: The term homogamy may be used either as a descriptive or as an explanatory concept. Employed descriptively homogamy means simply that there is a tendency for "like to mate with like," as has been demonstrated by the evidence just presented. Employed as an explanatory concept, homogamy is a term which accounts for a greater proportion than chance of marriages of persons of like rather than unlike characteristics.

In the judgment of the writers, homogamy is a descriptive rather than an explanatory concept. At least, there seems to be insufficient evidence to indicate any psychological impulsion of like to mate with like. In addition to association during engagement, certain factors in mate selection may be sufficient to account for the excess of unions of persons who are homogamous in social, physical, and personality traits.

Propinquity at school, church, work, and in recreational activities would undoubtedly favor engagements of persons of like social attributes. The image of the ideal mate derived from family and friends would probably, on the whole, also lead to mate selection of like with like particularly in social and physical characteristics.

The above factors, however, would not explain the small preponderance over chance expectation found in the homogamy of couples in personality characteristics. This excess may be due to the influence of parental image on mate selection. The tendency of young people to choose a mate with the personality characteristics of one or the other parent or of both parents has already been stated. If a son or daughter resembles one or both parents in one or more personality characteristics and also tends to select a mate with the same traits, the result would be a higher than chance expectation of the engaged couple having the same traits.

The indubitable fact of the homogamy of the fiancé and of the fiancée seems not to result from any impulse of like to mate with like but from the influence of association in engagement and from certain factors in mate selection—propinquity, image of ideal mate, and parental image.

Summary and Conclusions

Engaged couples are seldom able to state why they fell in love with each other. A careful analysis of interview and statistical data however revealed the nature and role of certain factors influencing their choice of a mate.

The first of these, propinquity, was found to be an essential condition, but in only a few cases the precipitating factor. Young people did tend to become engaged with those whom they first met at school or college, in the same recreational and work groups, and so on. Propinquity is therefore mainly a circumscribing factor, providing the spacial limit, social as well as physical, of the contacts that may finally eventuate in marriage.

Like propinquity, the image of the ideal mate in terms of cultural characteristics seems to be a limiting factor, excluding those whom a young man or woman would not consider as prospective wives or husbands. Of all the persons of the opposite sex whom a single person knows only a few qualify as possible marriage partners according to the standards, conscious and unconscious, of the ideal mate. Desired physical traits attract initially, but generally are not binding. The choice of a marriage partner depends more crucially upon his possession of valued personality characteristics.

Parental image appears to be a positive factor in mate selection. The father image for the daughter and the mother image for the son seem to influence the choice of a spouse. But the resemblance is considerably less in physical traits than in personality characteristics. Perhaps also the likeness is not as much in personality attributes as in the same or similar type of affectional and emotional relationship with the love object and the parent of the opposite sex. Finally, as indicated earlier, the parental image takes different manifestations. Probably, the person in the choice of a mate is influenced not by one but by both parents and through those characteristics which were most significant for his emotional development.

Personality need appears to be even more important than parental image in mate selection. Actually it often includes the latter. In addition it embraces unsatisfied wants arising from other experiences. What is necessary in the understanding of mate selection is to establish the existence of the need and not its origin. The central question in courtship and engagement then becomes the determination of the personality needs of the engaged persons and how completely and satisfactorily they are being filled.

When parents arranged marriages, social and economic status was the chief criterion of a successful marriage. In the old-time rural community economic standards, such as the farming ability of the young man and the housekeeping aptitude of the prospective wife, were given main attention. With marriage now in the control of young people, their adjustment to each other in fulfilling personality needs in a companionship relation becomes their chief concern in mate selection.

Homogamy is an intriguing aspect of mate selection. It is probably an interesting outcome rather than a significant factor in choosing a mate. The study of 1000 engaged couples confirms the findings of previous studies that in many physical, psychological, and social characteristics the tendency of like to mate with like is greater than that of opposites to be attracted. So far not a single instance of the reverse has been established. Interesting as is this fact, it does not imply that people have an homogamous impulse. The factors already considered—propinquity, image of the ideal mate, parental image, and personality need combined with family and social pressures—are all that seem to be needed to explain the preponderance over chance of homogamous unions. This assumed finding should, however, be demonstrated by research.

SELECTED BIBLIOGRAPHY

BARNETT, LARRY D., "Interracial Marriage in California." *Marriage and Family Living* (November, 1963), pp. 624–27.

BELL, ROBERT R., "Some Factors Related to Coed Marital Aspirations." *Family Life Coordinator* (October, 1962), pp. 91–94.

BURCHINAL, LEE G., "Research on Young Marriages: Implications for Family Life Education." *Family Life Coordinator* (September, 1960), pp. 6–24.

HEISS, JEROLD S., "Premarital Characteristics of the Religiously Intermarried in an Urban Area." *American Sociological Review* (February, 1960), pp. 47–55.

MARCHES, JOSEPH R., and TURBEVILLE, GUS, "The Effect of Residential Propinquity on Marriage Selection." *American Journal of Sociology* (May, 1953), pp. 592–95.

PAVELA, TODD H., "An Exploratory Study of Negro–White Intermarriage in Indiana." *Journal of Marriage and Family* (May, 1964), pp. 209–11.

PRINCE, ALFRED J., and BAGGALEY, ANDREW R., "Personality Variables and the Ideal Mate." *Family Life Coordinator* (July, 1963), pp. 93–96.

SNYDER, ELOISE C., "Attitudes: A Study of Homogamy and Marital Selectivity." *Journal of Marriage and Family* (August, 1964), pp. 332–36.

STRAUSS, ANSELM, "Personality Needs and Marital Choice." *Social Forces* (March, 1947), pp. 332–35.

THOMAS, JOHN, "The Factor of Religion in the Selection of Marriage Mates." *American Sociological Review* (August, 1951), pp. 487–91.

WINCH, ROBERT F., *Mate Selection*. New York: Harper & Row, Publishers, 1958.

PREMARITAL SEXUAL STANDARDS IN AMERICA

Ira L. Reiss

In attempting to study sexual behavior, it is necessary to take into account two types of social forces, varying in their degree of interrelationship. The "verbal" forces, which include what people believe or say they believe to be appropriate, are reflected in values, attitudes, and norms. The "behavior" forces are what people actually do in given social situations. In terms of complete social control, the "ideal" situation would be complete acceptance of values by all individuals both verbally and behaviorally; however, this "ideal" is never reached even in the most totalitarian society. The reality of social situations clearly shows that there may be verbal acceptance of values but that actual behavior may differ in degree to the extent that it may be the complete opposite of the verbalized values. This is not to suggest that behavior contrary to the general verbalized values of what is appropriate does function without an influential

Source: Pp. 218–22, 227–35 from PREMARITAL SEXUAL STANDARDS IN AMERICA by Ira L. Reiss. Reprinted with permission of The Macmillan Company.

symbolic value system. There are values that influence the behavior of many individuals and that are based on subcultures or other groups within the broader society. Therefore, it is doubtful that deviant behavior represents rebellion or rejection of social values at all levels of social interaction. Rather, the rebellion often represents conformity to the particular values of a group, and it is the values and/or behavior of the group that represents deviancy from society at large.

What are the various influences operating today concerning beliefs about premarital sexual behavior? One, and possibly the most important, is the sexual liberalism associated with increased education. We would also suggest the great importance of the age-peer groupings, keeping in mind that the peer-group associations of the young usually reflect the general values of society and, more specifically, the values, implicit and explicit, of the modern family. The influence of adolescent and young adult peer groups could become strong only as other agencies of society, especially the family, provided the social setting for it to do so.

Most parents continue to take a strongly restrictive view of sexual behavior to apply to their unmarried children. What has changed over time is that the restrictive forces are now based less on effective means of social control and more on feelings of shame and guilt. Very often parental control through shame or guilt is ineffective because the young person has values that are based on peer-group interaction and that do not define sexual behavior as his parents do. In effect, what many parents are saying to their young adult offspring is that deviant behavior will result in shame and guilt for them, the parents. Even if the young person is emotionally committed to his parents, it is unlikely that the force for conformity is a strong one.

The increasing importance of the peer group in influencing the boy-girl relationship fits the emerging nature of the modern conjugal family. The peer-group patterns fit the ethos of romantic love and the ego-need stress in courtship and mate selection that emerged as traditional family control over mate selection decreased.

This shift in the nature of courtship from a family-based elimination process to a series of personal involvements reduced the symbolic importance of premarital virginity in courtship. It is quite probable that, as the family's influence over mate selection weakened, the factor of female chastity came to be of less importance.

In the following selection, Reiss moves from his historical analysis to examine the possible trends of sexual standards that might be expected in the United States. Reiss's book does not report a specific study, but represents an objective compilation and analysis of studies by various other researchers. One basic function of all scientific research is its potential use for hypothesizing or making projections as to expected trends for the future. Reiss—drawing upon the research of Kinsey, Terman, and others—does an outstanding job of synthesizing and projecting on the subject of premarital sexual values and behavior.

The key events of the last few centuries were the numerous revolutions . . . —the urban-industrial, romantic-love, and feminist revolutions. These three revolutions were really one. A mighty change was occurring in Western society—a change more significant than any since the great discovery of agriculture ten thousand years ago. America and the Western World were changing into a new type of society, an urban-industrialized society. Because of this change, premarital coitus is not the same today as it was one hundred years ago. Its consequences and meaning today are quite different. Many people have not yet realized this, for the old beliefs about coitus tend to become reified.

Many of our problems in America today are due to the fact that we are operating, in certain respects, with our ancient rural customs in an urban-industrialized society. There is nothing wrong with these customs as such, but many of them do not fit our present-day society. The early agricultural societies ten thousand years ago must have faced somewhat the same sort of conditions. In those times, it would have been the older hunting-society norms which would be hanging on and causing problems. This emerging type of society is quite new, less than four centuries old, so we still remember quite a bit about our agricultural-rural past. We have, however, forgotten mostly everything about our hunting-society past. In a few centuries, the same may be true of much of our agricultural past. We will have devised many new norms, kept some of the old, and reshaped many others to fit our changing needs. The customs which are still capable of maintaining society, of helping to keep our culture unified and strong should last. In many areas of behavior, such customs are lacking, and new ones will have to be developed if we are to maintain cohesion. In the area of premarital sexual activity, many of our older customs can no longer do their job of maintaining our courtship institution, and new customs, such as permissiveness with affection, the transitional double standard, and petting with affection, are evolving. When one looks at these changes in the setting of the totality of events which have occurred in our society, they are not at all surprising.[1]

THE DOUBLE STANDARD AND ABSTINENCE

The revolutions have all tended towards equalitarian relations between men and women and were thus opposed to the double standard. It is unlikely that these revolutions will stop altering our society in this direction. Our society is too much a part of these revolutions. A rural society with its close-knit groups and strong social controls, with its non-rational approach and its lack of pragmatism is the ideal setting for the double standard. But that way of life is disappearing in America, and, as it departs, it is taking with it the double standard. The transitional double standard developed in the

[1] For an informative account of our agricultural revolution 10,000 years ago see V. Gordon Childe, *Man Makes Himself* (New York: Mentor Books, 1953). For an equally insightful view of the changes which have occurred with the advent of civilization see Robert Redfield, *The Primitive World and Its Transformations* (Ithaca, N.Y.: Cornell University Press, 1953).

attempt to somewhat liberalize the double standard to make it fit better into our society. At present this subtype seems to be growing rather than decreasing. However, it is possible that as people become more aware of the typical double standard inequalities still within it, it may lose some of its popularity to a single standard, such as permissiveness with affection.

Our way of life today emphasizes the full enjoyment of life by both men and women. We have a hedonistic approach to living, not an ascetic one. We are a nation of people who value rationality quite highly. We are so imbued with the scientific ethics of our time that we seem to demand that one be able to defend his views, whether they be in politics, religion, or in sexual morality.[2] The inequality of our traditional sexual customs and the many inconsistencies in men make them a good target for rationalism. The asceticism of these sexual standards is opposed by our hedonism and secularism.

However, the orthodox double standard is still very much with us. The fact that many millions of people reject it and would prefer another standard does not in itself remove this ancient belief. It has five or more millenniums of tradition to support it and it has the usual fear of the unknown to prevent people from leaving it. Many people probably have other preferences over and above the orthodox double standard, but most of these people are afraid to step out of line and they still have some amount of sympathy for this standard.[3]

This sort of attitude seems to be a frequent prelude to social change. The present-day situation indicates that the social supports of this way of life are greatly weakened, and more and more people

[2] For a most insightful analysis of these characteristics and others of our society, see Robin M. Williams, Jr., *American Society* (New York: Alfred Knopf, 1956). See especially chap. xi, "Value Orientations in American Society," pp. 372–442.

[3] In 1956, I asked one hundred of my students how they felt about the double standard, and over 90 per cent of them said they would prefer another standard, but many added that they would go along with the double standard since they did not want to try to "change the world." This is evidence of both the strength and the weakness of this standard.

are finding it distasteful. It is just a matter of time, then, until the reaction becomes somewhat stronger and people move more openly in other directions. The first innovators, in fact, have already appeared in the form of the adherents of the two single permissive standards, and in the supporters of the transitional double standard. In the meantime, do not be fooled; the "monster" is not dead. He is very much alive in the sexual customs of America—but the signs of his incurable illness are equally undeniable.

The trends in the standard of abstinence are quite similar to those in the double standard. . . . Abstinence has lost adherents because its ancient supports have been greatly weakened, e.g., the risk of pregnancy, venereal disease, social condemnation, and guilt feelings are quite different in present-day society. Also, the emphasis on the desirability of physical and psychic satisfaction is higher today. The concept of behavior which is acceptable to this standard is changing also. Our petting standards are mainly outgrowths of the unchaperoned dating period starting before World War I and are clear reflections of the more liberal, less controlled form of behavior among young people, which was and is a reflection of the new type of society which is developing. In this sense, it may be said that as the total number of adherents of abstinence decreased in the last fifty years, the relative number of adherents who accept petting as part of their standard of abstinence increased greatly.[4]

This sort of change in abstinence is what one would expect to occur in a society which was becoming much more open in its attitude towards sexual behavior and was also becoming freer and more equalitarian in its treatment of young people.[5] Such a change

[4] Kinsey and Ehrmann found that well over half of all virgins petted. Thus, our estimate of about half acceptance of petting seems to be a conservative one. Furthermore, some of the petting rates, such as petting to orgasm have doubled and tripled with those born after 1900, indicating the trend about which we are speaking. See Table 1 in this chapter.

[5] An interesting study of the sexual behavior of ministerial students today can be found in Austin L. Porterfield and H. Ellison Salley, "Current Folkways of Sexual Behavior," *American Journal of Sociology,* LII (November, 1946), pp. 209–16.

fits in perfectly with the over-all movement towards more sexual freedom for young people. It is in accordance with the tremendous increases in premarital coitus. In short, allowing increased sexual freedom to those who accepted abstinence was necessary if that standard was to continue to be significant in our culture. If the abstinence standards continued to allow only discriminate kissing, the number of adherents of such standards would probably have been drastically reduced. Such an event would have forced many people to choose coitus in preference to such rigid restrictions. This, however, did not occur, because there was an alternative; one did not have to choose between kissing or coitus; one could compromise and engage in petting. This is the choice many young people made. In this way they could gain increased sexual behavior and still keep their virginity. There have been suggestions made that we accept petting to orgasm for young people, as a compromise solution to our premarital sexual problems today:

> It seems that the solution most in accordance with modern knowledge lies in an intelligent giving of advice to adolescents, through the parents and through the ordinary channels of sex education, about the forms of sexual play that are most likely to lead to orgasm for both parties, and least likely to result in conception or an undesirable carryover into adult practice, coupled with a definite social tolerance of such equivalents as will enable them to be open and not clandestine.[6]

Nevertheless, there are many aspects of such a compromise which make it precarious. One quite obvious one is that petting is close enough to actual coitus so that it may easily tempt one to cross the line in behavior and eventually in belief also. This would be particularly true for those who accept heavy petting. These petting standards may be only stopping-off points on the way to a fully permissive standard. Many women, upon falling in love, seem to leave their petting standard and accept permissiveness with affection

[6] Alex Comfort, *Sexual Behavior in Society* (New York: The Viking Press, 1950), p. 99. Needless to say, Mr. Comfort is an Englishman.

or the transitional double standard. There is some evidence to support this transitory view of the petting standards. Between the ages of twenty and twenty-five, Kinsey found that the number of nonvirgins virtually doubled. Most of these women seem to accept their changed behavior without regret. It is probable that this is the time when the majority of the conversions from abstinence to permissiveness with affection or the transitional double standard occur. The transitional double standard is another subtype which, like petting,

Table 1: Accumulative Incidence of Petting to Orgasm among Females

	DECADE OF BIRTH			
Age	*Before 1900*	*1900–9*	*1910–19*	*1920–29*
14	1%	1%	1%	1%
16	3	5	6	6
18	6	10	13	18
20	10	17	22	28
25	15	30	34	43
30	24	39	45	—
35	26	44	53	—

SOURCE: Kinsey, *Human Female,* p. 275. The younger generation of males experienced a small increase in petting to orgasm. Kinsey, *Human Male,* p. 406. For the college-educated males, by ages 20 and 25, the respective percentages experiencing petting to orgasm are 37 per cent and 53 per cent for the older generation; 48 per cent and 62 per cent for the younger generation.

Accumulative incidence is *not* the same as cumulative percentage figures. The accumulative incidence percentage shows "the number of experienced persons in each age group, in relation to the number of persons in each group who are eligible for such experience." *Human Male,* pp. 115–18. Thus, in this table, at age 20, for those born before 1900, the rate is 10 per cent. This means that of all the women born before 1900 who were 20 years of age or over and who were unmarried at age 20 (this is the total eligible population), 10 per cent had experienced petting to orgasm by age 20.

developed in response to the liberal, permissive pressures of the twentieth century. This standard may also be only a temporary compromise on the road to a single standard of permissiveness, such as permissiveness with affection.

The following tables list some of the evidence for increased heavy petting and for the rapid rise in both petting to orgasm and actual coitus, between the ages of twenty and twenty-five.

Many people may be bothered by such a prediction of the increasing decline of the double standard and, more importantly,

Table 2: Accumulative Incidence of Premarital Coitus for Females

	DECADE OF BIRTH			
Age	*Before 1900*	*1900–9*	*1910–19*	*1920–29*
13	1%	1%	1%	1%
15	2	2	3	4
20	8	18	23	21
25	14	36	39	37
30	26	53	48	—
35	35	56	54	—

SOURCE: Kinsey, *Human Female,* p. 339. The percentage with experience goes even higher at older ages, but for our purposes, the most significant changes are the vast increases in the twenty to twenty-five age group. This is the time when many girls fall in love or become engaged. Such experiences appear to change their attitudes toward sexual intercourse. The younger generation of males, at the younger ages, had a small increase in the amount of coitus. See Table 5 in this chapter.

abstinence. But it cannot be denied that abstinence has declined since 1900, and there has been a strong shift in the direction of more sexual liberty for virgins. Furthermore, it cannot be denied that our society, with its lack of chaperonage, its anonymity, its rationality, its freedom for young people, and its equalitarian aspects, is not conducive to chastity. The main support today for both abstinence and the double standard is the emotional backing these standards derive from being taught as acceptable or proper behavior. People will think up reasons if they are asked why they behave a certain way, but emotional habit seems to be the valid explanation. Such emotional backing is potent and difficult to change regardless of other factors. One can see this in the reaction of American smokers to the lung cancer "scare." Although the American Cancer Society has come out against heavy cigarette smoking, most people continue to smoke and make up rationalizations for their behavior. The habits of years are hard to change. This is probably the major reason why abstinence and the double standard are still powerful despite all the forces which are slowly weakening them.[7]

As the double standard weakens, the choice more clearly becomes abstinence or permissiveness for both men and women. The double standard protected abstinence from this choice in the past, by affording a means of "evading" or "compensating" for full abstinence. Thus, although abstinence believers may dislike the double standard, it has been the main support of at least female chastity and of at least a formal allegiance to full abstinence. As equalitarian pressures weaken the orthodox double standard, it becomes more obvious that full abstinence for both men and women is not attractive to many Americans, and when forced to choose between full abstinence or greater female permissiveness, these people often choose permissiveness.

. . . . .

THE SINGLE PERMISSIVE STANDARDS

The revolutions were much kinder to the single standards. As urban living, reinforced by contraceptive knowledge and feminist pres-

[7] One area of the double standard which would likely repay investigation is that of pregnancy. It is in our folklore (witness, *Streetcar Named Desire*) that often it is during a woman's pregnancy that her husband commits adultery. The lack of sexual relations during late pregnancy and the lack (at times) of desire on the part of the pregnant female may be responsible here if this is a valid pattern. Such a situation seems to support the double standard unless love becomes a factor which helps control the man and encourage the woman to be more satisfying to the man.

sures, began to move society into a more equalitarian position, the permissive standards began to grow. After all, if society is changing in the direction of greater equality among the sexes, it is natural to expect the development of such single standards allowing equal sexual rights to both men and women.

It was in the iconoclastic environment of the 1920's that the permissive standards took root. The generation of people born between 1900 and 1910 revolutionized our sexual customs. The generations born since that time have somewhat continued these changes, but for the most part, they have only consolidated the inroads that this older generation perpetrated. Those born in the 1900–09 decade vastly increased our former sexual rates in almost all areas when they came to maturity in the 1920's—the decade of the sexual revolution. For the first time in history, women were given a chance for a third choice, i.e., it no longer was the Greek choice of Hetaerae or wife, or the nineteenth-century choice of pleasure-woman or wife; women could now choose to accept premarital sexual behavior, not as prostitutes or pleasure-seekers but as lovers.

Let there be no misunderstanding about the 1920's. Many people were just enjoying prosperity and bootlegging and having a fling. These people were not looking for a new sexual standard; many lacked any strong standard. The rapid changes in our society had uprooted these people and left them somewhat disillusioned or indifferent to sexual standards. Many were armed with the new freedom ideology of Freud and were waging war against the Victorian restrictions still present in our culture. They had no clear-cut standard—they were simply against repression of any kind.[8] Nevertheless, these people started the changes which eventually led to the growth of these standards. People do not like to feel guilty about

[8] The situation in the 1920's seems to fit Merton's description of anomie or normlessness. There was great pressure to engage in sexual relations and yet no acceptable way. The result was that rebellious and innovating responses occurred and we had the great sexual explosion of the 1920's. Robert K. Merton, *Social Theory and Social Structure* (Glencoe, Ill.: The Free Press, 1957). chaps. iv and v.

their behavior. Thus as time went on, many of these iconoclasts began to accept and formulate more liberal standards which would tolerate their behavior.

The following tables present evidence from our major research studies which documents this vast increase in premarital coitus and indicates the direction of these increases.

Tables 3, 4, and 5 contain much valuable information, but

Table 3: Premarital Coitus of Men and Women by Decade of Birth

	DECADE OF BIRTH		
	Before 1890	*1890–99*	*1900–9*
HUSBANDS			
None	50.6%	41.9%	32.6%
With Fiancee Only	4.6	7.6	17.2
With Fiancee and Others	9.2	23.0	33.7
With Others Only	35.6	27.5	16.5
	100.0	100.0	100.0
NUMBER OF CASES	(174)	(291)	(273)
WIVES:			
None	86.5	74.0	51.2
With Fiance Only	8.7	17.7	32.7
With Fiance and Others	2.9	5.8	14.0
With Others Only	1.9	2.5	2.1
	100.0	100.0	100.0
NUMBER OF CASES	(104)	(277)	(336)

SOURCE: L. M. Terman, *Psychological Factors in Marital Happiness* (New York: McGraw-Hill Book Co., 1938), p. 321. The fiance(e) referred to here is the person eventually married.

please bear in mind that the most that can be obtained from these studies is an indication of general behavior for certain segments of our population. The vast increase in sexual behavior, brought about by those people born between 1900 and 1909, is clearly illustrated in the tables. The male non-virginity figures are low on Table 3 because of the high number of male college graduates involved in this particular study. As mentioned previously college men seem to have the least amount of premarital coitus. This can also be seen in Table 5. Unfortunately, the part of Table 3 on men and Table 5 are not comparable, since Table 3 has no men in the birth category of the "younger generation." However, the general average of all the men in Table 3 and the college-educated men in the "older generation"

Table 4: Premarital Coitus of Women by Decade of Birth

	DECADE OF BIRTH			
	Before 1900	*1900–9*	*1910–19*	*1920–29*
None	73.4%	48.7%	43.9%	48.8%
With Fiance Only	10.4	24.4	23.3	27.3
With Fiance and Others	10.4	21.0	25.6	17.4
With Others Only	5.5	5.4	7.0	6.5
Incomplete Data	.3	.5	.2	.0
	100.0	100.0	100.0	100.0
NUMBER OF CASES	(346)	(610)	(896)	(627)

SOURCE: The data for this table were furnished the author by the Institute for Sex Research, thanks to the kindness of Dr. Gebhard and Dr. Martin. It was contained in a letter to the author dated February 23, 1960. The word fiance here means the man eventually married. The table is based on 2,479 "ever married" women. Part of the data can be found in Kinsey, *Human Female,* chap. viii, and all of the cases are from this volume. Table 5 presents what data are available on males. Precisely comparable data are not available.

in Table 5 are comparable. The males in Table 5 (older generation) are not broken down to check for trends within this group. In Table 3, such a breakdown is made into three decades and sharp trends are evidenced. Later increases in male non-virginity, as in the "younger generation" are slight and at certain ages only.

There are more recent data from the Terman study that could have been added to Table 3. These data indicate that 86 per cent of the men and 68 per cent of the women born between 1910–

19 were sexually experienced before marriage, but this information was based on only 22 men and 60 women, and I have not included it.[9] The Burgess and Wallin study is composed almost exclusively of couples born between 1910–19 and they report no such rapid rise in non-virginity.[10] Further, evidence for doubting this part of the Terman study can be obtained by examining Tables 4 and 5 which shows that Kinsey, like Burgess and Wallin, found no sharp rise in this decade.

In what kind of intercourse have these people engaged? In Table 3 the number of female virgins decreased from the "before 1890" to the "1900–09" birth group by a considerable amount, from 86 per cent to 51 per cent. Better than two-thirds of this decrease was due to increases in the number of women who had intercourse with their fiances only; the other one-third of the increase was due to women who had intercourse with their fiances and also with others. Kinsey's findings in Table 4 are somewhat more indicative of an equal growth in the "fiance and others" category as well as the "fiance only" category. But both of these categories indicate that there has been a tremendous increase in the number of women who are engaging in premarital coitus with their future spouses. Some of the "others" would be love affairs, while some would be more casual affairs.

Table 3 affords information on men over the course of several decades. An interesting set of changes appears to have occurred in this group of young men. Going from those born before 1890 to those born between 1900–09, we find there is an extraordinary reduction in the number of men who have premarital coitus of the "only with others" type. The percentage of men engaging in such behavior was more than cut in half. In the same period, the number

[9] For a statement of this finding, see L. M. Terman, *Psychological Factors in Marital Happiness* (New York: McGraw-Hill Book Co., 1938), p. 321.

[10] Burgess, Ernest W. and Paul Wallin, *Engagement and Marriage* (New York: J. B. Lippincott Co., 1953), p. 330. The general findings here were in accord with the tables presented. Roughly 46 per cent of the females and 68 per cent of the males were non-virginal in this study.

of men who had experience only with their fiancees increased almost fourfold. The increase in the number of men who experienced coitus with their "fiancee and others" was almost as great. Kinsey also notes this decrease in "only with others," when he mentions that about 10 per cent of the total premarital coitus of all the men in his study was with prostitutes, and, although the total amount of coitus did not decrease, the frequency of coitus with prostitutes seemed to have been cut in half in the younger generation described in Table 5.[11]

Table 5: Accumulative Incidence of Premarital Coitus for Men by Generation and Education Level

	EDUCATION LEVEL: 13 YEARS OR MORE		EDUCATION LEVEL: 0–8 YEARS	
Age	*Older Generation (Born before 1910)*	*Younger Generation*	*Older Generation (Born before 1910)*	*Younger Generation*
12	.5%	1.1%	2.5%	10.1%
14	6.3	5.9	20.8	34.8
16	14.9	15.6	48.1	66.8
18	27.0	31.4	73.3	81.9
20	38.8	45.4	82.2	86.6
22	48.2	55.8	83.3	85.9
25	62.0	65.9	90.3	88.9

SOURCE: Kinsey, *Human Male,* pp. 400, 404. Data on those males whose education stopped after 9–12 years of schooling, are not available for these generations. *Ibid.,* p. 550, shows over-all data for these high-school-educated groups which indicates that their frequency falls in-between the above two groups, *e.g.,* by age 16, 58 per cent were experienced, by 20, 75 per cent and by age 25, 84 per cent.

The older generation here refers to those males who came to maturity between 1910–25 and thus were born before 1910. This table only goes to age 25 in each generation but the rates for older unmarried males goes up only slightly. There is no data on the males' type of partner comparable to the female data.

[11] *Human Male,* pp. 300, 416, 599, 603, and chart on p. 410.

The over-all evidence from Terman clearly indicates that men, too, have experienced a most radical increase in the amount of sexual intercourse with their future spouses. The great decrease in the number of men who experienced coitus "only with others" is evidence of a significant change, i.e., the decline of the double standard. Men who formerly would not have coitus with their fiancees because they were "good" girls were now altering their standards and indulging with their fiancees. This probably meant that these men were either accepting the transitional subtype or were rejecting the double standard altogether and accepting permissiveness with affection in its place. Here, then, was a general movement in which men stopped being so strictly double standard and women ceased being so strictly abstinent.[12] Person-centered coitus was coming of age.

The similarity between these tables, composed of data gathered from people from different parts of the country, in studies separated in time by about fifteen years, lends support to the belief that these findings reflect a genuine trend in our culture. One should, however, be aware of the high percentages of college graduates and urban people in these studies. Although these are the best studies available, they are not fully representative and are subject to criticism on several levels, as was pointed out previously. They are, however, accurate enough to indicate general trends among large segments of our over-all population.

The lack of any sharp upswing in these trends since the peaks were established in the 1920's is hypothesized as due to a consolidation process. It might well be that, since the 1920's, what has been occurring is a change in attitudes to match the change in behavior of that era. The actual behavior may thus be very much the same, but a much larger percentage of these people today are

[12] Another study of similar age groups which also found the tendencies shown here is Harvey J. Locke, *Predicting Adjustment in Marriage* (New York: Henry Holt and Co., 1951), see especially pp. 136–37 and chap. vii *passim*. Note that in the Terman and Kinsey studies, although there have been vast increases in non-virginity, the percentage of non-virgins who indulge only with their future spouse remains almost the same.

people who no longer look upon their behavior as wrong and have more fully accepted person-centered coitus and petting.

It is worth noting that, although rates for coitus do not seem to have sharply increased since the twenties, the rates for petting have increased notably since then. (See table 1.) As has been mentioned, this increase in petting adherents may well lead, in time, to an increase in people who accept full coitus. It seems plausible to expect the change from abstinence to occur gradually and for individuals to accept petting before they fully accept coitus. This is one of the senses in which the time from the 1920's to the 1960's can be viewed as a consolidation process, a consolidation of the changes made and a preparation for further changes. In addition to the number of people who accept petting there seems to have been an increase in the transitional double standard, which also seems like a step toward a single standard of permissiveness with affection.

The 1920's were unusual times. Women were being arrested for wearing too-short bathing suits, men were being put on trial for teaching evolution, and bold girls were accepting the new ideas concerning petting and discussing sexual behavior with their dates. Out of this setting came the people who were to smash the sexual idols of Victorianism beyond repair. Compare our attitudes today to the 1920's and one can see immediately that, although our coital behavior is not radically different, we have consolidated our ideas and accept our behavior with a more natural, normal air. We are more sure of our beliefs.[13] There is still much confusion in the area of sexual beliefs today. But there are strong signs that the air is clearing, and, as the "clouds" move away, one can see the battered orthodox double standard and abstinence structures along-

[13] Kirchwey, Freda (ed.) *Our Changing Morality* (New York: A. and C. Boni, 1924), chap. by Leavenworth. This chapter was written in the 1920's, and one can see how chaperonage and the "evils" of divorce were much more current then. For an article written in the thirties on the changes in the twenties, see: Theodore Newcomb, "Recent Changes in Attitudes toward Sex and Marriage," *American Sociological Review,* II (December, 1937), 659–67.

side the new edifices of the standards allowing person-centered petting and coitus.[14]

My impression from my informal questioning of college and non-college people lends strong support to the research evidence quoted here.[15]

SELECTED BIBLIOGRAPHY

BELL, ROBERT R., "Parent-Child Conflict in Sexual Values." *Journal of Social Issues* (April, 1966), pp. 34–44.

BELL, ROBERT R., *Premarital Sex in a Changing Society*. Englewood Cliffs, N.J.: Prentice-Hall, Inc., 1966.

BELL, ROBERT R., and BLUMBERG, LEONARD, "Courtship Intimacy and Religious Background." *Marriage and Family Living* (November, 1959), pp. 356–60.

BELL, ROBERT R., and BLUMBERG, LEONARD, "Courtship Stages and Intimacy Attitudes." *Family Life Coordinator* (March, 1960), pp. 60–63.

14 The most recent evidence on the growth of person-centered coitus is in the . . . study by Winston Ehrmann. Ehrmann found that about one-half of the males and a smaller, though significant number of females accept intercourse when engaged. Ehrmann also found that if a girl was in love with her date, the chances of intercourse occurring were over three times what they were if no love was present. Ehrmann, *Premarital Dating Behavior,* chaps. v and vi.

15 Of course, a person's attitude cannot be discovered by simple direct questioning such as "What do you believe in?" Many people have not analyzed their own beliefs and do not fully know in what they believe. Others would answer differently depending on how well they knew the interviewer. The person who is asked "Is it right to go to church on Sunday mornings?" may well answer "Yes" because he has been taught that this is the proper answer, but he himself may only attend a few times a year and feel no qualms about it. So it is with people answering sexual questions. Most of them will give a recital of norms they have been taught. One must probe deeper and possibly use "projective" techniques such as asking their opinion of a hypothetical case of sexual behavior. This projective approach was used in my questionnaire study of high school and college students. For a most interesting discussion of interviewing see: Kinsey, *Human Male,* chap. ii.

BELL, ROBERT R., and BUERKLE, JACK V., "Mother and Daughter Attitudes to Premarital Sexual Behavior." *Marriage and Family Living* (November, 1961), pp. 340–42.

CHRISTENSEN, HAROLD T., and CARPENTER, GEORGE R., "Timing Patterns in the Development of Sexual Intimacy: An Attitudinal Report on Three Modern Western Societies." *Marriage and Family Living* (February, 1962), pp. 30–35.

DEDMAN, JEAN, "The Relationship Between Religious Attitude and Attitude Toward Premarital Sex Relations." *Marriage and Family Living* (May, 1959), pp. 171–76.

EHRMANN, WINSTON, *Premarital Dating Behavior*. New York: Holt, Rinehart & Winston, Inc., 1959.

KANIN, EUGENE J., "Male Aggression in Dating-Courtship Relationships." *American Journal of Sociology* (September, 1957), pp. 197–204.

KANIN, EUGENE J., "Premarital Sex Adjustments, Social Class and Associated Behaviors." *Marriage and Family Living* (August, 1960), pp. 258–62.

KANIN, EUGENE J., and HOWARD, DAVID H., "Postmarital Consequences of Premarital Sex Adjustments." *American Sociological Review* (October, 1958), pp. 556–62.

KINSEY, ALFRED C., POMEROY, WARDELL B., and MARTIN, CLYDE E., *Sexual Behavior in the Human Male*. Philadelphia: W. B. Saunders Co., 1948.

KINSEY, ALFRED C., POMEROY, WARDELL B., MARTIN, CLYDE E., and GEBHARD, PAUL H., *Sexual Behavior in the Human Female*. Philadelphia: W. B. Saunders Co., 1953.

KIRKENDALL, LESTER A., *Premarital Intercourse and Interpersonal Relationships*. New York: Julian Press Inc., 1961.

PRINCE, ALFRED J., and SHIPMAN, GORDON, "Attitudes of College Students toward Premarital Sex Experience." *Family Life Coordinator* (June, 1958), pp. 56–60.

REISS, IRA L., "Sexual Codes in Teen-Age Culture." *The Annals* (November, 1961), pp. 53–62.

REISS, IRA L., "The Scaling of Premarital Sexual Permissiveness."

Journal of Marriage and Family (May, 1964), pp. 188–96.

REISS, IRA L., "Premarital Sexual Permissiveness Among Negroes and Whites." *American Sociological Review* (October, 1964), pp. 688–98.

REISS, IRA L., "Social Class and Premarital Sexual Permissiveness: A Reexamination." *American Sociological Review* (October, 1965), pp. 747–56.

HUSBANDS AND WIVES

Robert O. Blood Jr. and Donald M. Wolfe

Probably no other society, past or present, has been more concerned socially and personally with marriage than that of the United States today. All of the mass communications media devote time and energy to questions about modern marriage, and much of their interest is directed at various "problem" areas of marriage—marital frustrations and unhappiness, sexual maladjustment, role confusion, divorce, and so forth. And of course, these and other areas have been of interest to various social scientists involved in studying the institution of the family.

It has been shown by anthropological research that the institutions of marriage and family may vary from society to society, each adapting according to its needs. While all societies throughout history have had some form of marriage, some societies have required that they be monogamous, while others have not. The insistence upon marriages being permanent may also vary with the society, as does the requirement that the husband and wife live together.

Source: Pp. 239–67 from HUSBANDS AND WIVES by Robert O. Blood Jr. and Donald M. Wolfe. Reprinted with permission of the Macmillan Company. © The Free Press, a Corporation, 1960.

Nor do the married couple always serve as the main source of their own livelihood or even as the source of the care, protection, discipline, and legal identification of their children.

In the American middle-class family of today, there is a strong belief in marriage being a relationship of togetherness. That is, in the United States, marriage generally has come to involve a high degree of intimacy and sharing between husband and wife. The couple attend social functions together and usually own their house, car, and other possessions jointly. This extent of marital sharing is usually not found in other societies, and it was not common to the American family of the past.

Also important, and peculiar to marital values in the United States, is that the successfulness of the husband-wife relationship generally is considered to determine the family stability and the success of family procreation. Our American ideals represent what approaches a cultural extreme, both in the reduction of family size and in the great value placed on the success of the marriage relationship. Even with the many changes undergone by American marriage, and even with the increased availability of divorce, the institution of marriage in the United States appears to be increasing in strength. In fact, American marriage rates are among the highest in the world; and, currently, the proportion of single people in the United States is at the lowest point since the start of the twentieth century. While in 1900, two out of every three women in the total population of the United States had been married at some time in their lives, at the present time this is true for four out of every five women. And over ninety per cent of all Americans will be married at least once before they die.

Most studies of the various aspects of marital interaction have been centered around middle-class and higher-educated husbands and wives. One of the values of the Blood and Wolfe study, part of which is reprinted here, is that the population studied was selected through the procedure of multi-stage probability sampling. The study was the culmination of extensive interviews with 731 urban and suburban wives in the Detroit area and with 178 farm

wives living in a rural section of Michigan. One problem with this study is that the interviewing was limited to the wives, thereby leaving it open to question as to whether or not husbands might define various marital situations somewhat differently from their wives. But this study is of great importance because of the sophistication in the design for the study as well as in the selection of the sample to be interviewed. The reading that follows is taken from the chapter where Blood and Wolfe assess the strengths and weaknesses of American marriages.

DISAGREEMENTS AS STRESSES

As evidence of the stresses [in American marriages], we will study marital disagreements. These are not the only source of weakness in marriage. Sometimes couples drift apart, no longer drawn toward each other by any positive attractions, no longer dependent on each other for essential services. Such might be called decaying marriages, in which the meaningfulness of interaction departs, or interaction itself gradually ceases. Such loss of vitality can be seen in marriages from which the wife derives little satisfaction. If her needs are not being satisfied, why should she go on living with this man? Especially if some other man might offer a better chance or at least a new chance of meeting her needs. The usual American attitude is that marriages dead from lack of nourishment should be buried in divorce—life is too precious to be wasted in meaninglessness.

Other divorces, however, result from repeated battles between husband and wife. They may belatedly discover incompatible philosophies of life or irritating personal habits. New issues may arise from changing circumstances, posing problems that couldn't have been solved in advance of marriage. Disciplinary issues for children, what to do about financial set-backs, whether and how to get rid of boring visitors—there are endless new questions in married living which couples may see eye to eye on—or may not.

Disagreement isn't necessarily fatal. Some divergence is normal in any marriage. More crucial is what happens from there on out. Most couples achieve some agreement, or agree to disagree. Usually someone gives in or a compromise emerges.

Only a few couples are chronically unable to settle their arguments. In Detroit, 2 per cent of the wives say that no agreements are reached when they differ with their husbands, that neither partner gives in. Equally rare is total failure to reach agreement in farm families. For such marriages, disagreements are disastrous. Every additional issue alienates the couple further. Each disagreement is an open sore that never heals.

For most couples, disagreements are less threatening. Nevertheless, the kinds of issues which plague a marriage often reflect its weakest points.

Major Issues in City and Country

What are the main issues which crop up in modern marriages? Table 1 indicates the areas covered by answers to the question, "Since you were married, what are the main things you and your husband have sometimes disagreed about?"

With few exceptions, the proportions of couples disagreeing about general topics are similar for city and farm families. Only when specific issues within topical areas are examined, do farm problems differ from city problems.

Table 1 shows that financial problems crop up in more marriages than any other category of disagreement. The proportions of city and farm families involved are practically identical, but their financial problems differ considerably when examined in greater detail. Urban disagreements are heavily concentrated around criticisms of the partner's extravagance, prices paid for particular purchases, and housing decisions. Rural Michigan wives move so seldom that housing is rarely an issue. Their chief disagreements reflect more difficult economic decisions, most often involving purchase of a major durable item, what the family can afford or will have to do without, and priorities for purchases. Often these rural issues involve struggles between the vested interests of the husband and the wife. Every expensive piece of farm machinery means postponing improvements for the house—and vice versa. In such a context, it is likely to be difficult for partners to compromise because their points of view differ so much.

The greatest conflict over children for both farm wives and city wives involves discipline. Child-rearing inevitably raises questions about how strictly the children should be handled—questions which differ little from city to country.

Recreational issues split into two main types: differing tastes in leisure-time activities and disagreements about the amount of companionship the partners have together. The latter is a typical feminine complaint because of the wife's need to get out of the home

Table 1: Major Areas of Disagreement in Urban Families

	NUMBER TABULATED	
Type of Disagreement	*Chief Disagreement*	*Total Disagreements* *
Money	24%	42%
Children	16	29
Recreation	16	30
Personality	14	28
In-laws	6	10
Roles	4	7
Religion-politics	3	4
Sex	†	1
None	15	15
Not ascertained	2	2
TOTAL	100	168 ‡
NUMBER OF FAMILIES	731	731

* Most wives typically mention two areas of disagreement, while a few mention three or four. The right-hand column shows the total of all disagreements mentioned in each category, giving a rough idea of the proportion of all couples who ever have a major disagreement in that area. The first-mentioned disagreements are used as the basis for comparison in subsequent tables.

† Less than ½ of 1 per cent.

‡ Total adds to more than 100 per cent because many wives gave more than one response.

for a change of scenery. The chief rural obstacle to companionship in recreation is the husband's heavy work responsibility. When combined with physical isolation, this makes the farm wife twice as apt to complain of inadequate social life as the city wife (11 per cent vs. 5 per cent). She is so desperate for recreation that almost any activity will do—at least she disagrees with her husband about *what* to do less often than about the need to do *something*.

City husbands, too, are sometimes preoccupied with work responsibilities, but more apt to engage in separate recreation, leaving the wife to stew at home (5 per cent vs. 1 per cent). The fact that the husband is away from home during the day gives him contacts and friendships alien to the wife, which tend to involve him in after-hours activities apart from her. Sometimes this means coming home late from work because he has had some fun with "the boys." Other times, he goes out after supper to rejoin them. At least the farm wife has the advantage of being able to accompany her husband in his leisure time pursuits—if he can find time for any.

Personality clashes take many forms, only one of which differs by place of residence. City couples more often quarrel over acts or habits of one spouse which are morally disapproved by the other (6 per cent vs. 2 per cent for farm couples). Drinking and running around with other women (or men) are typical examples of this. The rural-urban difference could mean that rural consciences are better able to resist temptation. More tangible is the fact that rural environments present fewer temptations. The same separation of work-place from residence which causes urban husbands (and sometimes wives) to get involved in separate recreational activities also involves them in separate delinquencies. Indeed, except for the partner's moral disapproval, these delinquencies could be classified as recreational disagreements. What makes the husband come home late from work may just as well be a drink with the boys in the one case as in the other. If the wife disapproves of his drinking, the disagreement goes down as a personality issue. If she resents only his preferring the boys to her own company, the issue is recreational.

The journey to work is not the only urban factor in marital

delinquency. The size of the community also contributes. In a small town, the average man is known by almost everybody, and this network of primary relationships reinforces his superego. In a large city (Detroit has two million people), the anonymity of the crowd invites deviant behavior unsanctioned by gossip. The big-city husband may feign work at the office while taking his young secretary to a show or cocktail lounge, and unless the wife's grapevine is unusually effective, nobody except the two delinquents will ever know the difference. Some urban escapades therefore fail to provoke conflict at home because they are unknown to the wife—but enough alcohol on the breath, lipstick on the collar, and mysteriously disappearing money become apparent to cause appreciable difficulty. Nor are husbands the only urban delinquents—wives, too, are sometimes influenced by the attractions and distractions of the urban environment, the more so as *they* journey to work.

Even more personality clashes, however, center around differing tastes, irritating (but not immoral) personal habits, temperamental quirks, and back-seat-driving-type criticisms of the other's skill. Such issues arise as often in the country as in the city.

The remaining problem areas affect so few families that they can rarely be meaningfully subdivided. Role conflicts involve the wife's working (in city or country) and the division of labor in the home. City wives alone accuse their husbands of not working hard enough, not earning enough money, or otherwise neglecting their role, and some wives in both city and country come in for criticism about their housekeeping.

"Religion-and-politics" is mostly religion in both city and country. Ten per cent of the farm couples but only 3 per cent of the city couples report a major disagreement at some time or other about what church to go to, how often to go, or some other aspect of religion.

As for sex, not a single farm wife ventured to mention this private subject to our interviewers, despite the fact that most of the interviewers were married women. The handful of city wives bold enough to specify this area of disagreement unquestionably leads to an underestimation of the amount of sexual conflict in the general population. A better estimate might be secured by using a list of topics to be checked. Left to their own initiative, however, respondents probably hesitated to utter the three-letter word.

What about wives who say they never disagree about anything worth reporting? Are they hiding something? A few of them may be, but by and large they are consistent. In answering a related question, none of them says she and her husband disagree more often than other couples, and most of them say they disagree less often than others. Having no disagreements doesn't necessarily mean the best of all possible marriages; but, turned the other way around, it is safe to say that, in good marriages, disagreements get solved with relatively little difficulty.

Sources of Trouble

Disagreements may reflect characteristics of the wife alone, the husband alone, or the relationship between the two of them.

Table 2: Disagreements, by Education of Wife

	EDUCATION OF WIFE		
Disagreement	*Grade School*	*High School*	*College*
Money	17%	26%	18%
Children	16	19	21
Recreation	13	15	16
Personality	17	15	18
In-laws	3	7	2
Roles	2	4	12
Religion-politics-sex	4	3	5
None	28	11	8
TOTAL	100	100	100
NUMBER OF FAMILIES	147	391	62

EDUCATED SENSITIVITIES: Table 2 shows two ways in which the wife's education affects her disagreements. One is her readiness to report disagreements. Not a single wife among twenty-four college *grad-*

uates fails to report at least one area of disagreement, and education generally is associated with fewer reports of no problem areas. It may be inferred from the rest of this book that such a relationship does not mean that education ruins women for marriage (despite ancient fears). Rather, college alumnae are probably less apt to keep quiet when they disagree with their husbands, more anxious to work things through to a settlement, and more apt to recall such disagreements when interviewed subsequently.

Women who went only to grade school may have fewer disagreements because they are less verbally-oriented. Another factor involved is their greater average age. All women past fifty tend to report few disagreements, perhaps because they have been married so long. By that time disagreements have often been settled and forgotten, or else communication between the husband and wife has dwindled off, reducing the danger of disagreeing (or agreeing) about anything.

While educated wives tend to report more disagreements in general, they especially often disagree with their husbands about marital roles. Those who have been to college appear to be sensitive about the question of women's roles and to push for idealized husband-wife roles.

MONEY, MONEY: Disagreements about money are most pronounced among high-school educated wives. This may be primarily a question of income. Wives with only a grade-school education are usually married to husbands whose incomes are too low to offer much choice in how to spend it. Thus, only 19 per cent of city couples with below-average incomes have had memorable disagreements about money. Unlike farm families with equally little money (who have to make difficult choices between farm equipment and household expenditures), most city families face routine decisions about keeping the bills paid and the larder full. It takes at least a five-thousand-dollar income, apparently, for money to acquire live options in the city; 37 per cent of the disagreements of six- to seven-thousand-dollar-income couples are financial. Such couples have more than enough to subsist on, but not an inexhaustible supply of money—so financial choices loom large. Only above ten thousand dollars does the supply of money become generous enough to reduce financial disagreements to a low 9 per cent. In part, this reduction is achieved at the expense of increased complaints by the wife that the husband's "busy-ness" in making this money deprives her of his companionship.

HETEROGAMY: Quarrels over personal habits tend to occur in certain types of marital relationships. If the husband has had much more education than the wife, she seldom (11 per cent) mentions personality conflicts. However, as the balance of education shifts in the opposite direction, the percentage of disagreements rises steadily to a peak of 25 per cent when the wife has had at least three more years of schooling than the husband. When a man marries such a woman, he is likely to be in for considerable criticism from her about his uncouth ways.

Religious disagreements are more common in interfaith marriages than in homogamous ones, but not as much so as might be expected (6 per cent vs. 3 per cent). Personal criticisms loom largest (23 per cent) among couples who attend different churches at differential rates. Usually, it is the wife who is religious and the husband who seldom goes to his alien church, making him especially liable to criticism for his irreligious behavior.

ROLE PROBLEMS: Table 3 reveals the role problems of working wives. Many of these couples undoubtedly disagree about the wife's employment itself. In addition, that employment requires drastic reshuffling of marital roles, most notably in the division of labor. This is reflected in the fact that couples who share the most household tasks have not the least but the most role disagreements. When the wife's employment involves both partners in overlapping responsibilities for household tasks, role conflicts are apt to occur. Questions of how much each partner should do crop up because of the lack of boundaries between tasks. In most households, such disagreements are settled by allocating tasks unilaterally in a specialized division of labor—but the time shortage of double-employment couples requires coparticipation at home with recurrent potential stress.

Table 3 also suggests that overtime work by the husband tends to cause disagreements over lack of companionship, but to reduce disagreements about money.

Table 3: Disagreements, by Comparative Work Participation of Husband and Wife

	Comparative work participation		
	WIFE NOT EMPLOYED	WIFE EMPLOYED	
Disagreement		*Husband Overtime*	*Husband Full-time*
Money	23%	17%	27%
Children	21	17	11
Recreation			
a. Conflicting *interests*	10	11	16
b. *Amount* of companionship	5	6	2
Personality	15	15	15
In-laws	6	4	5
Roles	3	8	8
Religion-politics-sex	4	2	2
None	13	20	14
TOTAL	100	100	100
NUMBER OF FAMILIES	443	53	65

The differences between working wives and housewives in disagreements over children are a function of the number of children the latter have to care for. This can be seen more clearly in life cycle changes.

CHANGING PROBLEMS: From the previous discussion of working wives, one might expect role conflicts to be common among new brides, a majority of whom are working. The fact that none at all occur among our twenty "honeymoon" couples illustrates the extent to which working has become an accepted role for young women without children (see Table 4). With two incomes and no dependents, their money worries are few. Such couples are still at the dating stage as far as their main roles in life are concerned, disagreeing not

Table 4: Disagreements, by Stage in Family-life Cycle

	STAGE IN FAMILY-LIFE CYCLE						
Disagreement	*Honey-moon*	*Pre-school*	*Pre-ado-lescent*	*Adoles-cent*	*Post-parental and Retired*	*Un-launched*	*Child-less Couples*
Money	10%	28%	24%	23%	21%	23%	18%
Children	—	13	29	32	10	20	—
Recreation							
a. Interests	20	8	8	9	6	—	14
b. Amount	10	9	5	7	11	3	6
Personality	20	14	16	11	14	23	12
In-laws	15	8	5	2	2	3	10
Roles	—	5	4	4	4	5	4
Religion-politics-sex	10	4	3	3	5	2	4
None	15	11	7	10	26	22	31
TOTAL	100	100	101	101	99	101	99
NUMBER OF FAMILIES	20	130	140	101	97	65	49

about who should do the minimal housework but about what movie to see.

In-laws are an issue when the partners are young—indeed the younger the wife, the more often conflicts over relatives are mentioned. As young adult men and women transfer their loyalties from their parents to each other, some stress is inevitable and it shows in the concentration of in-law problems at the beginning of youthful marriages.

The biggest differences in Table 4 are between young couples without children and those with young children on their hands. If ever a transition from one life-cycle stage to another is a crisis, this is it. Suddenly the wife's employment shifts from being taken for granted to being controversial. Most wives, of course, quit work. The few who continue working under financial pressure tend to criticize their husband's economic incompetence, while the occasional middle-class career woman is apt to be criticized by him for neglecting her maternal and housekeeping tasks.

Money jumps into first place as a problem when the wife quits her job to have a baby. Belt tightening to accommodate reduced income and increased expenses requires choices that husband and wife may disagree about. The standard of living isn't necessarily worse at this point (dissatisfaction tends to intensify as more children are added and they develop more expensive appetites). Rather, the drastic shifts in income and expenditures require the most rethinking now.

As noted above, husbands who work overtime may provoke disagreements about the lack of joint recreation. During early childbearing, the complaints in this area undoubtedly reflect the wife's feeling of being tied down by dependent young children.

Children themselves do not become the chief bones of contention until they are old enough to get into "deliberate" trouble. Between the ages of six and eighteen, disciplinary questions are liable to divide the husband and wife even more than financial questions. Beyond age eighteen, children who still live at home become more responsible for themselves and create fewer issues for parents. They even become for many wives a substitute source of gratification, reflected in the rarity of disagreements about companionship in the unlaunched group. However, wives who no longer find their husbands very useful are still apt to snipe at them for personality deficiencies, the more so because of the gap between the two partners.

In the postparental period, the problems of companionship reassert themselves as joint use of leisure time resumes (or at least the wife wishes it would!). Also, the approach of death makes religious questions take on a new interest.

An unusually large proportion of the permanently childless couples report no disagreements whatsoever, reflecting the smooth continuity of their pattern of living. When they do conflict, they resemble childless "honeymoon" couples in disagreeing pre-eminently about their leisure-time dating.

MARITAL INTERACTION PATTERNS: Couples who disagree about companionship are not necessarily uncompanionable. Couples interested in recreation enough to disagree about it usually manage to get in a good deal of it as measured by frequency of joint activities. Despite this, they are least satisfied with the companionship they get, else they wouldn't disagree about it so much. They are not therefore objectively deprived couples but dissatisfied in relation to high expectations.

The two young wives who confess to disagreements about sex have highly companionable marriages. Least companionable are couples who disagree primarily about money. Sex is an interactive matter whereas money is a question of objects outside the interpersonal relationship—hence the differential relationship to companionship.

Highest on mental-hygiene functioning are wives who have no disagreements (because their husbands understand them so well?). However, they wish they had more companionship. Advice and active help are given most often to wives plagued with child-rearing problems. Least therapeutic are the relationships between husbands and wives who attack each others' personalities. Such wives are especially apt to get critical responses if they share their troubles with the husband after a bad day.

The Impact of Disagreements on Marriage

Rated especially incohesive are marriages where in-laws are a problem. Such marriages are usually in the early stages of being glued together.

When wives are asked how often they have disagreements, those whose chief problem is children report the highest frequency. From year to year, children present ever new disciplinary problems to be solved.

Couples with role problems also feel that they have more disagreements than the average family. Nevertheless, they manage to have cohesive, satisfied marriages. This combination illustrates how stresses can be taken in stride by a good marriage. A marriage need not be devoid of disagreements to be strong.

However, few marriages can stand attacks on a partner's personal behavior without serious consequences. Such attacks loom large in the alienation which leads to divorce. Personal attacks hurt the ego too much to be easily repaired or easily forgiven. The damage they do lives after them to haunt attacker and victim alike. If any particular disagreements are symptomatic of crippling stresses in marriage, personality conflicts are the ones.

THE FREQUENCY OF DISAGREEMENTS: When Detroit wives were asked whether they disagree with their husbands more or less often than other families they know, most say less often. This is a logical absurdity—how can the average couple disagree less than the average couple? Nevertheless, a wife's answer to this question is symptomatic of her attitude toward her marriage and reflects a *relative* difference in the frequency of disagreements.

Wives who claim few disagreements are consistently more satisfied with the standard of living, the companionship, the understanding, and the love provided by their husbands. Conversely, the few wives who feel that they have more disagreements than other couples are conspicuously dissatisfied with their husbands. They also have the greatest discrepancies in their child-bearing experience, especially in the direction of unwanted children. Lack of enthusiasm for their children is partly a feedback from the unhappiness of their marriages, but the objective evidence shows that they average 2.34 children born compared to 2.19 for wives who claim average disagreement rates and 1.96 for those who disagree less than usual. In view of the fact that disagreements are most frequent among couples whose chief problem is children, it is difficult to escape the conclusion that children are a potent source of conflict between husbands and wives.

Frequency of disagreeing is also related to mental-hygiene functioning. Husbands who give advice and sympathy have the fewest disagreements, whereas critical husbands have the most. Correspondingly, wives who experience few disagreements find the husband's therapeutic response most effective, whereas feeling worse is associated with many disagreements. Perhaps these are different ways of saying the same thing—husbands prone to disagree are likely to throw the wife's complaints back in her face. In any case, disagreements are not a form of communication which wives prize. Rather, they are both causes and consequences of marital alienation. In general, disagreements prominent enough to stick in the wife's memory reflect genuine stress.

THE STRENGTHS OF AMERICAN MARRIAGES

How strong are the marriages in a metropolitan community and on nearby farms? How vital, how meaningful? Are they hollow shells on the verge of collapse? Are they vestigial appendages of a changing civilization, soon to be cast aside?

There are two ways of determining answers to such questions. One is to ask the participants themselves how they feel about their marriages, the main approach in this study. The other is to ask outside observers to pass judgment on what they see in the marriage. This, too, has been done using the sociologists-in-training who coded each interview schedule as the observers. The cohesiveness shown in the *behavior* (not the self-evaluations) of the respondents was rated in this fashion.

If there were serious discrepancies between the wives' stated satisfactions and the coders' ratings of cohesiveness, it might mean that one of the measures doesn't mean much. Actually, there is a high correlation between the two (87 per cent of the dissatisfied wives being rated incohesive compared to only 1 per cent of the most satisfied wives, for example). Such results testify, at least, to the consistency between verbalized satisfaction of the wives and the rest of their interview responses. More likely, they indicate that wives who say they are satisfied with their marriages are not bluffing but really mean it.

From this point of view, the satisfaction of the interviewed wives is impressive. The vast majority of marriages fulfill the participants' expectations. Although very few wives feel that their marriages can't be improved in any respect, the average wife is not far from such enthusiasm. The old slogan urged skeptics to "Ask the man who owns one." We asked the women who own contemporary marriages, and they proved to be satisfied customers.

The objection might be raised that unhappy wives are rare because they have already become divorcees. This is less of a factor than might be imagined. While more than one-sixth of all first marriages do end in divorce, divorcees remarry so fast that they tend to be interviewed in their second marriage. Five per cent of the farm women and 11 per cent of the city women interviewed were remarried divorcees. This high rate of remarriage prevents the U.S. Census from finding more than 3 or 4 per cent of adult women in American cities at any one time who are unmarried divorcees. This means that a relatively small proportion of the satisfaction of Detroit wives can be attributed to skimming the cream off initial marriages.

Taken as a whole, these contemporary marriages appear quite stable from the standpoint of the participants. People who are satisfied are not likely to change partners or to give up married life for living alone. Only the few dissatisfied marriages are vulnerable to enticement from without and disintegration from within. The rest of the marriages meet too many of the participants' needs to be sacrificed.

All contemporary marriages are not equally satisfactory, however, so it will be useful to conclude this exploration of the dynamics of married living by reviewing the major sources of strength in marriage. There are four: (1) the family's social status, (2) the couple's homogamy, (3) the extent to which they meet each other's needs, and (4) children—in moderation. Against these, must be set a counter-agent: the corrosion of time.

The Family's Social Status

An important source of marital satisfaction for the wife is the husband's prestige or social standing in the community. Undoubtedly, many wives feel proud to be married to a man who is socially prominent or respectable and embarrassed if the husband is looked down upon by others. However, that is not what is meant here by marital satisfaction. Rather this term refers to how satisfied the wife is with the way her marriage functions, with the extent to which her husband meets her needs for companionship, children, understanding, love, and a comfortable standard of living. When the wife reports how satisfied she is with her husband *as a husband,* she is not simply duplicating the community's assessment of him if she rates a high-status husband tops.

Table 5: Marital Satisfaction, by Social Status

	PERCENTILE RANKING ON SOCIAL STATUS INDEX				
	0–19	*20–39*	*40–59*	*60–79*	*80–99*
Marital satisfaction	4.45	4.59	4.70	4.65	4.93
NUMBER OF FAMILIES	11	80	198	178	88

Table 5 shows that high-status husbands do rate high with their wives. This means that the higher the husband's standing in the community the better he is able to play the role of husband. (Theoretically the wife's greater satisfaction could result from lowered expectations, too, but common-sense observation suggests that high-status couples expect a good deal of each other.)

The reasons why high-status marriages function so well can be illuminated by presenting the four component parts of the Social Status Index, namely the husband's occupation, income, education, and ethnic background.

Table 6 shows that education is most closely related to marital satisfaction. Occupation and income, on the other hand, although generally associated with satisfaction, incur slight declines in the upper brackets (occupation to a slight extent, income rather

Table 6: Marital Satisfaction, by Husband's Occupation, Income, Education, and Ethnic Background

Marital Satisfaction by			BLUE COLLAR		WHITE COLLAR	
Husband's Occupation:			*Low*	*High*	*Low*	*High*
			4.61 (155)	4.61 (165)	4.85 (81)	4.80 (155)
Husband's Income:		*Under $3,000*	*$3,000 –4,999*	*$5,000 –6,999*	*$7,000 –9,999*	*Over $10,000*
		4.32 (57)	4.75 (165)	4.80 (185)	4.61 (82)	4.72 (54)
Husband's Education:	*Some Grade School*	*Grade School Graduate*	*Some High School*	*High School Graduate*	*Some College*	*College Graduate*
	4.29 (62)	4.42 (78)	4.56 (124)	4.90 (182)	4.96 (55)	5.04 (51)
Husband's Ethnic Background (Major Groups):		*Negro*	*Polish*	*Irish*	*German*	*British*
		4.23 (105)	4.82 (77)	4.47 (49)	4.61 (79)	4.70 (135)

drastically). This difference suggests that a distinction must be made between settled, crystallized high status in which family position has been consolidated on a high plane for a generation back, and status currently being struggled for, through earning money the hard way at the expense of the marriage. If high income is earned through the husband's preoccupation with his job to the neglect of his wife, she feels dissatisfied. Indeed Table 6 suggests that comparatively little income is needed to satisfy the wife as long as it measures up to her expectations.

Education, by contrast, symbolizes a way of life involving a happy blend of companionship, love, understanding, and children, which at the same time provides an adequate standard of living without undue effort. These differences are analogous to the differences between aristocratic upper-upper class families and showy "nouveaux riches" but they extend well down into the middle class.

While its relation to satisfaction is not completely consistent, the prestige level of various ethnic groups depends to a considerable extent on the length of time they have been in the United States. Hence, marital satisfaction tends to be associated with the number of generations of American ancestry the couple have behind them (see Table 7).

Table 7: Marital Satisfaction, by Degree of Americanization

	DEGREE OF AMERICANIZATION			
	Both Partners Immigrants	*One Partner Immigrant*	*Minimally First Generation*	*Minimally Second Generation*
Marital Satisfaction	4.31	4.56	4.73	4.93
NUMBER OF FAMILIES	59	68	193	157

We believe that lengthy residence in the United States affects the family more by providing secure status in the community than by acculturation to American family norms. In any case, the process of Americanization doesn't seem to undermine family life as far as the participants are concerned.

To summarize, high social status provides a more satisfying marriage for the wife, insofar as it gives the husband the *savoir faire,* the emotional security, and the leisure to meet her needs, at the same time that he discharges his occupational role competently. Wives of men who are struggling to achieve such status can take comfort in the thought that their children will experience a more satisfying way of life than they have known. Families more moderately situated may find a pattern of living which suits their expectations eminently well. Dramatic evidence of this is the identical satisfaction scores of urban Detroit families and Michigan farm families who, on the whole, are far from prosperous. But bottom-status families, especially Negro families, are likely to find the going tough and married life just as dissatisfying as their life in the community. These are the weakest families in the community, most liable to divorce and desertion, for whom a satisfactory family life under adverse conditions is a rare achievement.

The Couple's Homogamy

How much a husband can satisfy his wife's needs depends not only on his standing in the community but also on his position relative to her. If his position is similar to hers, they tend to have compatible interests and expectations, and to share a common style of life. If his position is higher, he will be able to offer greater resources than she is used to which will partially offset the incompatibility of their backgrounds. However, if his position is lower than hers, the strain of incompatible outlooks is compounded by his inability to measure up to her expectations. Hence, homogamy normally produces the greatest satisfaction for the wife, husband-superiority gives lessened satisfaction, and husband-inferiority the least (see Table 8).

Usually, there is a limited range within which it matters little whether the husband and wife are precisely equal or differ slightly. This is especially true of age, since minor age differences signify little in terms of differential resources or differing interests. Moreover, the norm of current American practice is for the husband to be several years older than the wife—hence this "normal" group is the most satisfied maritally. Unlike superiority in education or occupational background, superior age is no guarantee that the husband will be able to offer the wife greater resources to compensate for differences in friends, interests, energy levels, etc. Indeed, since aging is so highly associated with declining marital interaction, an older spouse is very apt to function less adequately.

The mean scores regarding comparative education fit the theory of compatibility perfectly. Presumably, more extreme differences in education would depress satisfaction still further.

Other data show that marked superiority in the husband's occupational background increases rather than decreases the wife's satisfaction. Such husbands are able to offer sufficiently greater resources of family background, style of life, and money to offset the strains involved in a mixed class marriage. While the wife benefits from a discrepancy in this direction, correspondingly lessened satisfaction may be predicted for the husband.

Table 8: Marital Satisfaction, by Comparative Age and Comparative Education of Husband and Wife

	HUSBAND SUPERIOR		EQUAL	HUSBAND INFERIOR	
Marital Satisfaction	*Markedly*	*Slightly*		*Slightly*	*Markedly*
By Age *	4.23 (35)	4.74 (193)	4.79 (256)	4.65 (57)	4.00 (14)
By Education †	4.55 (93)	4.73 (115)	4.89 (180)	4.62 (94)	4.51 (71)

* Cutting points for age differences are as follows: husband 11 or more years older; 4–10 years older; 1–3 years older or equal; 1–3 years younger; and 4 or more years younger. Numbers in parentheses show the number of families on which means are based.

† The cutting point on education is 3 or more years for markedly different.

Religious differences are a source of strain which lacks the invidious distinctions of age and status differences. Table 9 shows that the greater the difference in religious backgrounds, the less the satisfaction.

To summarize these comparisons, homogamy seems to make it easier for two people to achieve a better marriage. If the husband is superior to the wife, his additional resources may be sufficient to make up for the incompatibility, but if he is inferior, the wife's satisfaction normally suffers from his inability to meet her needs and expectations.

Table 9: Marital Satisfaction, by Comparative Religious Background of Husband and Wife

	RELIGIOUS BACKGROUND		
	Same	*Mixed-Protestant*	*Protestant-Catholic*
Marital satisfaction	4.79	4.63	4.58
NUMBER OF FAMILIES	258	144	125

The Personal Needs Met by the Marriage Partner

Homogamy provides the foundation on which a strong marriage can be built. What the couple does with their potentialities determines how satisfactory the marriage really is. Thousands of people in the world are homogamous in age, education, religion, and social status, but homogamy alone doesn't guarantee satisfaction. Compatible individuals must go beyond choosing one another to loving each other and doing what love requires of them. Basically, love requires serving the partner in ways which satisfy his basic needs.

Marriage serves many needs—physical, emotional, and social. The following needs illustrate the contribution that particular services make to marital solidarity: (1) the need for self-esteem; (2) the need for companionship; (3) the need to be understood.

THE NEED FOR SELF-ESTEEM: Everybody needs to respect himself and to feel that others respect him. The restoration of self-respect is a prime goal of the mental-hygiene function in marriage. It is accomplished, in part, by ego-repair from the partner, after injury has occurred at the hands of someone (or something) else.

To be able to repair his wife's ego, a man must have a

sound relationship with her. He cannot be therapeutic if he offends her through neglect or ridicule.

But making a marriage work involves more than avoiding strain and providing therapy. Self-respect is also created through respect from the partner. Such respect is manifested through consultation over issues which concern both partners.

It is disappointing to discover that a major decision has been made without sounding out those involved. Unilateral moves produce feelings of not counting, of being a nonentity. By contrast, it is invigorating to feel that one matters to someone else—and no high-sounding words can prove this as much as inclusion in the decision-making process.

Table 10 shows the conspicuous marital enthusiasm of wives

Table 10: Marital Satisfaction, by Decision-making Pattern

	DECISION-MAKING PATTERN			
	Husband Dominant	*Syncratic*	*Automatic*	*Wife Dominant*
Marital satisfaction	4.64	5.06	4.70	4.40
NUMBER OF FAMILIES	120	120	187	91

who are counted-in on decisions. Equality between husband and wife is not the crucial factor—for autonomic couples are just as equal but much less enthusiastic. Equality combined with separate decision-making is a kind of not counting, not mattering to the other partner in his area of interest.

What about the dominant wife—doesn't she count? In the sense of having a voice in decisions, she obviously plays an even more central role than a syncratic wife. What matters is whether she counts in the eyes of her partner—and this is precisely where dominant wives get short-changed. The reason for their dominance is the husband's abstention from the marriage. His marginality is evidence precisely of disrespect. Hence the wife who must "go it alone" in marriage feels dismayed rather than pleased.

The joint consultation of syncratic couples has instrumental value beyond undergirding the partners' self-respect. Decisions made jointly are most likely to represent the interests of both partners and therefore to meet other needs as well. Syncratic couples are likely to be unusually satisfied with the allocation of marital resources from the decisions actually made.

It is important to note in passing that there is a significant difference between sharing power and sharing tasks (see Table 11).

Table 11: Marital Satisfaction, by Sharing of Household Tasks

	NUMBER OF SHARED TASKS *				
	None	*One*	*Two*	*Three*	*Four or more*
Marital satisfaction	4.46	4.77	4.88	5.11	4.74
NUMBER OF FAMILIES	171	166	103	53	27

* Number out of the eight major household tasks on which the wives were questioned.

Being consulted in decisions is ego-reinforcing. Being helped with household tasks provides some companionship (and lack of mutual participation reduces satisfaction), but extreme sharing of this sort is not essential to knowing that one matters to the partner. Couples may specialize in tasks where each is most competent without feeling any loss of respect thereby. Indeed the recognition that one has a skill the partner lacks may be ego-enhancing in itself.

On the other hand, the decreased satisfaction which accompanies high sharing of home tasks probably doesn't result from sharing as such but from the stressful conditions under which pervasive help becomes necessary. Usually it is couples pressed for time by joint employment, many young children, etc. who share so much—and their marital satisfaction is impeded by the same stress-producing factors.

Some sharing of tasks is required for maximum satisfaction. The optimum pattern is neither complete sharing nor complete separation, but help as needed. Consistent sharing in work, then, is not essential to feeling respected. But shared decision-making is essential to mutual respect.

THE NEED FOR COMPANIONSHIP: People need people. Lack of contact with others is one of the symptoms of severe mental illness. But companionship is something more than just being near others. It involves appreciation for the presence of a particular person. It is the added enjoyment which comes from sharing experiences with a close friend, and the added satisfaction which comes from knowing that one's own presence is valued, too. The desire to spend life together is the essence of marriage. Cemented by religious and legal ceremonies, by social supports and inner functions, marriage is the most effective means ever devised for meeting man's need for companionship.

The close relationship between marital satisfaction and companionship reflects the high value which most wives place on this particular aspect of marriage (see Table 12).

Joint participation in organizations characterizes satisfied couples, provided it is not carried to an extreme. Similarly, it is not necessary for husband and wife to possess all friends in common or to be always on the go in visiting and entertaining. The most satisfying pattern seems to be a variety of leisure-time activities, many but not all of which are shared together. There is still room in a companionable marriage for freedom and independence as well as for sharing and togetherness. In fact, companionship in interaction with outsiders (organizational, colleague, and friendship) may reduce satisfaction when carried to extremes.

On the other hand, there is no saturation point in communicating separate experiences to each other. Such communication keeps the two partners abreast of each other's development. The fact that the partner takes time to share his thoughts and experiences is further evidence of counting. But pure vicariousness is not enough. It takes shared information plus joint activities to provide an adequate sense of companionship.

THE NEED TO BE UNDERSTOOD: Companionship and shared decision-making are all very well when life goes smoothly. However, there

Table 12: Marital Satisfaction, by Type and Degree of Companionship

	DEGREE OF COMPANIONSHIP				
Type of Companionship	*None*	*Slight*	*Moderate*	*Considerable*	*Intense*
Organizational *	4.60	4.70	4.92	5.04	4.58
	(327)	(54)	(93)	(55)	(24)
Informative †	4.32	4.17	4.54	4.67	4.90
	(34)	(24)	(54)	(193)	(240)
Colleague ‡	4.46	4.75	—	5.11	4.80
	(212)	(186)		(103)	(50)
Friendship §	4.22	4.54	4.84	4.87	4.76
	(50)	(128)	(77)	(178)	(119)

* Number of joint memberships: none, one, two, three, four or more. Numbers in parentheses are number of families on which mean is based.
† Frequency husband reports work events: never, seldom, monthly, weekly, daily.
‡ Frequency of visiting work mates: never, seldom, monthly, weekly.
§ Proportion of husband's friends wife knows quite well: none, some, half, most, all.

are crises in life when what is needed is not just a companion but help in solving problems and a sympathetic ear. This is a more erratic need than the other two, important chiefly when setbacks occur, but contributing to marital satisfaction even in good times because of the memory of previous help and the secure knowledge that it is available as needed.

Table 13 shows the striking differences in marital satisfacfaction between marriages in which the wife's problems are understood by the husband and those in which she is unable to communicate her troubles to him or is rejected for doing so. Clearly, the most satisfaction is generated when the husband is attentive to and directly helps to solve the problems his wife faces. When this is not possible, sympathetic understanding and efforts to help the wife get out of difficult situations produce satisfaction. But husbandly passivity yields little help or promise for the wife, and critical or irresponsible reactions to the wife's difficulties tend to increase dissatisfaction. In short, when the husband responds positively, the wife's need to be understood is fulfilled. If he responds negatively or she fears that he would, her needs go begging.

Table 13: Marital Satisfaction, by Husband's Therapeutic Response

Husband's Therapeutic Response	*Marital Satisfaction*	*Number of Families*
Help solve the problem	5.27	32
Sympathy	4.94	170
Help withdraw from situation	4.90	20
Advice	4.74	107
Passivity	4.58	96
Dismissal	4.31	42
Criticism	4.17	35
Wife never tells him	4.34	48

Self-respect, companionship, and understanding are only a few of the needs which marriage is designed to meet. Insofar as a given marriage does so, it brings to the participants satisfaction, increased love, and lasting strength.

Children (in Moderation)

Children are a source of strength in marriage provided there are not too many of them. Children are like medicine—in proper doses they create health, but an overdose can be detrimental.

Both by the number of children ever born and by the number currently living at home, three is the magic number. Above three, satisfaction declines rapidly. This is related to the fact that (1) mothers of more than three or four children often wish they didn't have so many. This is not a universal reaction but occurs often enough to impair average satisfaction. (2) There is a rare but perceptible tendency for some women who are dissatisfied with their husbands to want extra children. Having more children makes them

Table 14: Marital Satisfaction, by Number of Children Ever Born and by Number Presently in Family

	NUMBER OF CHILDREN					
Marital Satisfaction	*None*	*One*	*Two*	*Three*	*Four*	*Five+*
By Number Ever Born	4.50 (80)	4.77 (140)	4.78 (171)	4.93 (96)	4.60 (43)	3.90 (29)
By Number Presently in the Family	4.32 (164)	4.67 (132)	4.86 (147)	5.16 (76)	—4.86— (37)	

happier personally, but doesn't make them any more satisfied with their husbands. (3) The kind of people who have large families are often those whose marriages are less satisfactory anyway. Low-status, poorly educated, immigrant women (to cite a few relevant groups) wouldn't have much more satisfactory marriages if they had fewer children—although it might help. This status handicap applies more to the older generation than to the younger, hence, the especially low-satisfaction rating of women who have borne more than four children (most of whom are too old to have that many still around).

Conversely, one reason why mothers of three children are so satisfied is that this is the number most often preferred by high status women. However, there is more to this business of numbers than just selectivity. Wives with many fewer than three children often feel unfulfilled and disappointed. Usually the fault is not the husband's, yet the wife's satisfaction with the kind of marriage she has is affected. More demonstrably, "extra" children strain the ability of the husband and wife to function as an intimate pair. The extra responsibilities, extra noise, extra expense, etc. tend to come between the partners. If they are not to neglect their children's needs, they must lose touch with each other to some degree. They can't have as much companionship, enjoy as many romantic evenings, take as much time to talk to each other because of the competing demands of the children.

This is not to say that they are necessarily any less happy. This may be just what they want. Most mothers of large families say they would have the same number over again if they had their choice. Indisputably, however, in having so many children they sacrifice the husband-wife relationship in favor of the parent-child relationship. They become family-oriented instead of marriage-oriented. Only within the limits of three or perhaps four children is it possible for an ordinary husband and wife to maintain effective communication with each other. Beyond this point perhaps a few couples succeed but the majority do not.

Children, then, are a source of strength in marriage—although not in every part of it or for every couple—up to a certain point. The point of diminishing returns in this particular sample is four. For other cities or at other times the precise turning point may differ. Doubtless in every modern community, some such turning point will be found, beyond which it's hard for a husband and wife to continue to see each other "across a crowded room."

The Corrosion of Time

Wearing away at the strengths in marriage is the corrosive influence of time. Table 15 shows how the average wife's marital satisfaction ebbs with the passing decades.

The first few years of marriage are a honeymoon period which continues the romance of courtship. With the birth of the first baby, satisfaction with the standard of living and companionship decline. In subsequent years, love and understanding sag, too. If children do not come, their absence is an alternative source of dissatisfaction.

These trends do not involve all couples, but affect a very large proportion of the total. In the first two years of marriage, 52 per cent of the wives are very satisfied with their marriages, and none notably dissatisfied. Twenty years later only 6 per cent are still very satisfied, while 21 per cent are conspicuously dissatisfied. These

Table 15: Marital Satisfaction, by Length of Marriage

	LENGTH OF MARRIAGE				
	Under 2 years	*3–9 years*	*10–19 years*	*20–29 years*	*30+ years*
Marital satisfaction	5.36	5.02	4.77	4.20	4.10
NUMBER OF FAMILIES	33	174	180	81	88

figures suggest that a majority of wives become significantly less satisfied in later marriage than they were at the beginning.

Some of this decline involves the calming of enthusiasm into satisfaction as a result of getting used to the partner, no matter how fine he may be. Newlyweds *ought* to be enthusiastic because they are tasting new satisfactions for the first time. However, much of the decline in satisfaction reflects observable decreases in the number of things husbands and wives do with and for each other. Hence, corrosion is not too harsh a term for what happens to the average marriage in the course of time. Too many husbands and wives allow their marriages to go to seed for any milder term to be appropriate. As individuals, middle-aged husbands and wives may find satisfaction elsewhere—in friends, the husband in his work, the wife in her children—they seldom find as much in each other.

OF TIME AND OF CHILDREN: The fate of marriage is not purely a question of time. Children can be another source of weakness or of strength, depending on how old they are and how many there are. Length of marriage, and age, and number of children are three inter-related factors embraced by the single concept of the family-life cycle (see Table 16).

At first, the arrival of children effectively offsets the corrosion of time. For one thing, marital satisfaction is heightened by the fulfillment of the universal desire to have children. Moreover, the children's impairment of the standard of living and of husband-wife companionship is offset by the increased sense of understanding and love which young mothers experience. Conversely, by the time childless couples have been married as many as four to seven years, the disappointment of hopes for children affects the wife's satisfaction so profoundly that tangible compensations like a high standard of living and continued dating companionship hardly dull the sense of tragedy.

Once the preschool stage of infantile dependency has passed (dependency of the child on its mother and of the mother on her husband in turn), declining satisfaction characterizes each succeeding stage in the family-life cycle. The only possible exception to this generalization is that there may be a second honeymoon of increased satisfaction for a brief period following the departure of the last child. Unfortunately, we cannot test this hypothesis with the present data, since we failed to ask when the launching occurred for post-parental couples. Even if we knew, there are historical complexities which might confuse the picture. Parents who completed their child-rearing in the 1950's were those whose child-bearing had been hampered by the Depression of the 1930's. Hence the child-bearing deficiencies concentrated in this cohort of wives artificially depress their over-all marital satisfaction.

Regardless of historical factors, it seems probable that the marriage relationship is eclipsed by other interests in the later years of child-rearing. This seems especially true of women with launchable children at home. Many families don't keep their children home past the nineteenth birthday. Their children go off to college or

Table 16: Marital Satisfaction, by Stage in Family-life Cycle

STAGE IN FAMILY-LIFE CYCLE [AMONG FAMILIES WITH CHILDREN]						
Childrearing stages		*Pre-school*	*Pre-adolescent*	*Adolescent*	*Un-launched*	
		5.22 (121)	4.95 (133)	4.59 (95)	3.96 (56)	
Childless stages	*Honey-moon*				*Post-parental*	*Retired*
	5.26 (19)				4.32 (77)	4.00 (8)
STAGE IN FAMILY-LIFE CYCLE [AMONG CHILDLESS COUPLES]						
Stages comparable to		*Pre-school*	*Pre-Adolescent*	*Adolescent*		
		4.55 (9)	4.32 (28)	4.11 (9)		

move into apartments with working friends or get married. It may be that having adult children at home is symptomatic of deviance. One hint in this direction is the tendency of mothers of unlaunched children to wish they had fewer children. Whether this is because they resent the child's failure to become independent or because they hold onto the oldest child to help support and care for a flock of unwanted younger siblings is not clear. Whatever the reasons, these wives have notably unsatisfactory marriages.

STRESSES AND STRENGTHS IN AMERICAN MARRIAGES

Compared to the prophecies of doom . . . , contemporary marriages sparkle. Most wives are satisfied with the love, the understanding, and the standard of living provided by their husbands. Moreover, economic prosperity and medical science may improve their ability to have the number of children they would like to have.

Weak spots there are—most notably in Negro marriages and to a lesser extent in low-status quarters generally. Incompatibility creates extra stresses when couples marry with major differences in age, education, religion, etc.

Nevertheless in any marriage, strength can come from meeting the needs of the partner to be consulted, to have companionship, to be understood—in short, to be loved. Strength ordinarily comes from children, too, except in those rare cases where children were not wanted or come in excess.

American marriages are particularly satisfactory in their early years—despite the fact that most divorces occur in the same years. In the midst of rearing children, the marriage relationship tends to be subordinated. However, it may retain enough vitality to reassert itself when child-rearing is completed. Moreover, lessened enthusiasm is offset by deepened habituation in the later years.

In any case, there seems to be little evidence, from the 909 wives interviewed, that American marriage as an institution is on the verge of collapse. On the contrary, as long as men and women continue to have important needs satisfied by their partners, marriage is "here to stay."

SELECTED BIBLIOGRAPHY

BABCHUK, NICHOLAS, "Primary Friends and Kin: A Study of the Associations of Middle Class Couples." *Social Forces* (May, 1965), pp. 483–93.

BERNARD, JESSIE, "The Adjustments of Married Mates," in Harold T. Christensen, ed., *Handbook of Marriage and the Family* (Chicago: Rand McNally & Co., 1964), pp. 675–739.

BUERKLE, JACK V., ANDERSON, THEODORE R., and BADGLEY, ROBIN F., "Altruism, Role Conflict and Marital Adjustment: A Factor

Analysis of Marital Interaction." *Marriage and Family Living* (February, 1961), pp. 20–26.

CUTLER, BEVERLY R., and DYER, WILLIAM G., "Initial Adjustment Processes in Young Married Couples." *Social Forces* (December, 1965), pp. 195–201.

DEUTSCHER, IRWIN, "The Quality of Post-parental Life: Definitions of the Situation." *Journal of Marriage and Family* (February, 1964), pp. 52–59.

FOOTE, NELSON N., "New Roles for Men and Women." *Marriage and Family Living* (November, 1961), pp. 325–29.

KIRKPATRICK, CLIFFORD, *What Science Says About Happiness in Marriage*. Minneapolis: Burgess Publishing Co., 1947.

LOPATA, HELENA Z., "The Secondary Features of a Primary Relationship." *Human Organization* (Summer, 1965), pp. 116–23.

PINEO, PETER C., "Disenchantment in the Later Years of Marriage." *Marriage and Family Living* (February, 1961), pp. 3–11.

BLUE-COLLAR MARRIAGE

Mirra Komarovsky

Over the years, there have been many studies of the various dimensions of marital roles and marital interaction. Most of the studies have been made with middle-class couples and have attempted to distinguish general patterns of values and behavior. From these studies, there have emerged general characteristics or criteria common to middle-class marriages that the couples themselves have defined as "successful." The selection that follows is a departure from the usual: it examines marriages in the "blue collar" class to determine what characteristics they may have in common.

To understand better the contrast this study found between marriages in the two classes, a brief description of the general characteristics usually found in middle-class marriages may be helpful. The first common belief is that marital satisfaction is frequently dependent upon the achievement or definition of individual marital roles. When a person enters a marriage, he is confronted with a range of possible behavior patterns within socially defined limits. There is generally no great threat to the individual's role so long as his behavior falls within the defined limits. However, problems may develop if his personal desires fall outside of what he or his spouse defines as appropriate role behavior. Sometimes, the individual who conforms to role expectations may feel a sense of personal frustration. In fact, few individuals do fill their marriage role for any length of time without some dissatisfaction with his own or with his spouse's role; but for most, role dissatisfactions are not crucial enough to define the overall marriage as unsatisfactory.

The second characteristic of middle-class marriage is that each partner in the marriage feels that he must have some opportunity to express his own personality. Sometimes in marriages, the role demands lead to a sense of personal frustration. The individual may feel that he never has the opportunity to develop personality interests of his own because the demands of the marriage roles are so overwhelming. In marriages, it is undoubtedly important that each have to do some things "not" shared by the spouse.

The third characteristic is that each marriage partner serves as an important focus of affection for the other. Because love in the middle class is the most important reason for getting married and because it is important in sustaining the marriage, the partners usually must be reassured continually that love exists. It is usually through the continuation of love and affection in marriage that the person maintains the feeling of being wanted and being important to the other. The reciprocal nature of the love relationship provides an important aspect of ego-need satisfaction for each partner.

Finally, each partner derives some pleasures and satisfactions from the marriage role relationships. Mutual satisfaction may be viewed as the opposite to the individuality discussed in the second point. That is, if some individual expression in marriage is needed, the couple also usually need to interact as husband and wife. If the individuals do not, their marriage roles will have little meaning since these roles derive their meaning and importance from the interrelationships of the husband and wife.

The selection that follows is the summary of Komarovsky's research; and, as such, attempts to put her findings within a theoretical framework. Studies of lower-class marriages are important as specific social class phenomena as well as for broader social class comparisons. The families that Komarovsky studied are not at the lowest social class level, but fall between the lower and middle social class levels. The importance of this "blue collar" group is shown numerically by the fact that in 1963 about 49 per cent of all employed whites and 80 per cent of all employed Negroes in the United States were in "blue collar" occupations.

Professor Komarovsky's method of study was to use case studies. She interviewed 116 persons who comprised fifty-eight married couples. A minimum of six hours was spent with each family unit, including two two-hour interviews with the wife and one two-hour interview with the husband. Therefore, one of the most important assets of this research is that it is one of the few studies of marriage where "both" husbands and wives participated.

The sample of 58 marriage relationships studied was made up of white, native-born citizens, whose parents were native born. The respondents were also Protestant, not over 40 years of age, and parents of at least one child. The social class designation of "blue collar" is based primarily on the educational and occupational levels of the husbands. Of the 58 husbands, 18 were high school graduates and 17 did not go beyond the eighth grade. By occupation, 18 of the men were "skilled," 22 "semi-skilled," and 10 "unskilled."

MARITAL DISORGANIZATION

The theory that illuminates Glenton's problems bears little resemblance to some dominant interpretations of social ills. In contemporary sociology, social problems are generally associated with anomie or the breakdown of social norms, cultural ambiguities and institutional conflicts.[1] * Relevant as these concepts are in a period of vast world changes, they may lead to an overemphasis upon consensus. Glenton's families are generally stable, respectable, and law-abiding, sharing deeply internalized and common values. Stable though they are, one-third of these marriages fail to rate our assessment of "moderately happy." In 14 per cent of the cases the marriages are "very unhappy." There is no doubt about this latter diagnosis; in these very unhappy cases all but one of the wives (and she was also wretched) voiced strong regrets about their marriages. Slightly over one-third of the marriages are rated as moderately happy. At the other extreme, slightly less than one-third are happily or very happily married. Their numerous problems will serve as a reminder that, if social ills are frequently the product of moral confusion, it does not necessarily follow that clear moral directives and consensus are synonymous with social health.

Some violations of social norms were no doubt concealed from us. Allowing for such under-reporting, the evidence nevertheless strongly suggests that deviant behavior plays only a minor role in the marriage problems of our respondents. Illegitimacy, adultery, juvenile delinquency, alcoholism, refusal on the part of the housewife and the provider to fulfill their obligations appear to be rare exceptions. The husbands are not all adequate providers but it is not for want of effort and devotion. There are many other examples, as we shall show, of failure to attain desired and culturally sanctioned goals but this failure does not generally lead to violations of legal or moral codes.

Social disorganization, however, may exist in the absence of deviant behavior.[2] The distinction between the two concepts proved its usefulness in the case of Glenton. Deviant behavior refers to violations of normative codes. Social disorganization, on the other

[1] See, for example, Robert K. Merton and Robert A. Nisbet, 1961, p. 13.

* Full documentation to references cited by Mrs. Komarovsky is given at the end of this selection.—Ed.

[2] See Robert K. Merton and Robert A. Nisbet, 1961, pp. 697–737.

hand, has been defined by Robert K. Merton as "inadequacies or failures in a social system of interrelated statuses and roles such that collective purposes and individual objectives of its members are less fully realized than they could be in an alternative workable system."[3] Social deviation may be one cause of disorganization but it is not the only one, and it must not be permitted to obscure the other causes. Moreover, the distinction between the concepts of deviation and disorganization enables us to raise significant problems as to their interrelationship. For example, what are the consequences of particular kinds and degrees of deviance for the ability of specified social systems to fulfill their goals? How do other deficiencies of social systems affect the patterning of deviance?

Social disorganization in Glenton is not the result of deviant behavior, nor yet of the other conditions strongly emphasized in current theory, i.e., institutional conflict and moral dissensus. Our respondents are relatively alienated from many institutions of the community. Having few institutional ties they are consequently spared the conflicts caused by competing demands of various statuses. For example, the familiar conflict between career and family life does not plague the workingman. His emotional investment in the job is relatively slight. Irregular work shifts occasionally create problems for the family but no workingman's wife need feel jealous of her husband's job and he himself does not feel guilty because his career leaves too little time for his family. The workingman's wife does not resent her husband's career but neither does she feel that she contributes to it by social entertaining or advice. The husband cannot count on her assistance but he is protected from critical scrutiny of his performance on the job.

Though rare, competing loyalties do exist. The union, the church, and a youth group each absorbed the interests of three men to the extent that their wives felt neglected. In two of these cases the marriage is problem-ridden and the wife sensed that her husband's preoccupation is motivated by the wish to escape the unhappy home.

Conflicts in marriage are sometimes created by the outside

[3] *Ibid.*, p. 720.

affiliations of the wives, several of whom are more active in churches and in clubs than their husbands. One man with ten years of schooling, married to an intelligent high school graduate, active in the affairs of her church, confessed to the interviewer:

"I might not have told you but she said she already told you, that nothing in the world gets me more than coming home and finding she's not here and not knowing where she is. I get to thinking, maybe she's out gabbing with the women in the church and that gets me mad and blue. She usually comes home in the middle of church suppers and things like that to fix my meal for me. I like that a lot. I think I'm an average man. I enjoy my family. A little untidiness is O.K., but if it's there all the time, you can't take it, *especially if it's because she has outside interests*" [italics ours].

Another woman, also a high school graduate, is active in the P.T.A. and in the church. The church has created the one serious problem in an otherwise happy marriage:

"He didn't want me to teach Sunday School. I cried plenty and it was a real problem in our marriage. It wasn't only the Sunday School. It grew into the teachers' meetings and afternoon services. He now feels a little more a part of it. They asked for volunteers to serve coffee during the coffee break at the church and he volunteered and had a good time talking to people. But he still doesn't like to go to church and still doesn't let me do everything I'd like to do."

Both of these men find their main gratification within the home whereas their wives are enjoying the heady wine of leadership in outside organizations. The first husband is patently dependent upon his wife. The irony of the second case is that the husband has succeeded in transforming his shy and insecure wife into a more outgoing person. She gives him full credit for this metamorphosis. But having become self-confident, she is reaching out into community activities. "He doesn't like to share me with anyone or anything"—all the more so, we might add, because he himself has no strong interest either in his work or in civic participation.

It is no accident that in both cases the wives are high school graduates. The latter exceed the less-educated women in church and club memberships. In our sample, the educated women also exceed their husbands in group memberships. The less-educated couples conform more closely than the high school graduates to the specialization of the roles posited by Talcott Parsons.[4] Among the former the husband is not merely the provider but the "secretary of state" concerned with the family's relations to the external world. But the high school wives tend to be more involved in community affairs than their husbands.

One problem caused by multiple affiliations is, however, quite prevalent. We refer to the in-law problems . . . that are created by continued interdependence of the married couple and their parental families.

Another allegedly prevalent contemporary problem is also rare among these families. Ambiguous definitions of conjugal roles or conflicts over different conceptions of marriage cause few marital difficulties because spouses have similar cultural backgrounds. The exceptions to this consist of a few cases of religious and class intermarriages.

The intermarriage that creates the more serious strain is one in which the wife (and not the husband) has the superior class background.[5] The marriage norms of the high blue-collar worker are more egalitarian than in the lower strata and the wife who marries "up" has no difficulty in accepting this improvement in her position. . . .

But when the high blue-collar woman marries "down," the consequences may be more stressful. A characteristic conflict of such a marriage concerns social life—especially as regards recreational activities without the children. "He likes us all to be together all the time and I'd like to leave the children home and have us do things by ourselves sometimes," said a mother of four children, a high school graduate who married "down." "Sometimes I think it's because he didn't have any education and he has nothing else to do

[4] Talcott Parsons, 1955, p. 47.

[5] See Julius Roth and Robert F. Peck, 1951.

or to think about than just relaxing at home with the T.V." The couple disagree about baby-sitters. The husband shares the frequently held attitude of low blue-collar families: "I wouldn't leave my children with a stranger." The wife, on the other hand, would prefer to pay a stranger instead of depending upon services given by relatives that she would have to repay. Social life is a bone of contention in still another way. The husband expects relatives to join in all the social entertaining but the wife considers personal congeniality on social occasions to take precedence over ties to kin. Education is another subject of disagreements in this family. The husband resents the money spent by his wife on the *Reader's Digest* and its series of abridged books. He does help the young children with their homework but frequently feels that chores around the house are more important than school work, while his wife emphasizes the latter.

The yearning for a more romantic approach to love-making was expressed by one 34-year-old high school graduate who married a rough, less-educated but benevolent patriarch. "I'd be happy if we'd just go along the road and park somewhere sometimes," she said. "What do you think you're doing?" he is likely to say, "we are too old for that kind of stuff." This is a restless, energetic woman with an inquiring mind, married to a good provider who likes his home and wants to be left alone to enjoy his comfort. She tries to stimulate and to rouse him but succeeds only in evoking a stubborn defensiveness. Their previously satisfactory sex life has been harmed by this psychological interplay. She is puzzled by his neglect of her. "It isn't that he doesn't respond, you touch him and he gets excited but he doesn't like to do that any more."

Other differences in class backgrounds of the spouses and the problems discussed so far are, to repeat, exceptional in Glenton. But these families pay a high price for their immunity to some typical ills of our time. This immunity is produced by their isolation from social mainstreams. But the shield that protects them from the disorganizing influences of social change is also a barrier against its benefits. Similarly, if they are spared the conflicting demands of various organizations they are also deprived of the advantages of social participation.

In turning now to Glenton's major problems we shall at the same time qualify the current emphasis upon institutional conflicts and the breakdown of moral consensus as the main source of social disorganization.

It is not the failure to maintain traditional social patterns but the failure to modify them that accounts for some marital problems in Glenton. In a period of rapid social change, effective socialization into traditional patterns may contribute to social disorganization.

The sharp differentiation of masculine and feminine roles and the absence of the expectation of friendship in marriage are cases in point. Even when fully accepted by both partners these cultural patterns create difficulties for each. The husband pays a price for his relative exemption from domestic duties. Irritability, the apathy, the desire for a job outside the home—these are the reactions of some women to the domestic routine unrelieved by companionship with their husbands. Mr. Daniels was not the only husband baffled by his wife's frequent depressions. He consulted a relative who told him that women are subject to fits of "neurasthenia." He could not perceive any connection between his neglect of his wife and her condition because he behaved in what was, for his group, the accepted way. Some situations create frustrations even when they do not violate any norms. The young wife who has no expectation of friendship in marriage can still feel lonely. The young husband who never expected a wife to share his interests can still experience boredom with her conversation.

The reader may cite the case of the Greens to show that marriages can be satisfying even when they are not based upon friendship. This is a fact worth noting. But such marriages require the availability of relatives and close friends. Geographical mobility tends to separate the married couples from kin and trusted friends. The Smiths are only one of several families that demonstrate the burden such separation places upon the marriage to provide the emotional support previously given by other primary groups.[6] The same lesson is implicit in the cases of the Greens and the Kings, whose satisfactory marriages depend upon functions performed for each spouse by outsiders. These older norms of marriage will become increasingly unsuitable if the following prediction by a government agency proves accurate: "Many more of our workers than in the past must have, or develop, the mobility to shift jobs. . . . Many may have to change their residence as well as their occupation."[7]

Traditional patterns have today other unfavorable consequences. Because the need for psychological intimacy could not be satisfied in marriage, some men and many more women exchange confidences with outsiders. But friendship has a dynamic of its own and cannot always be contained within the prescribed limits. Even in a marriage which is "not for friendship," the disclosure of certain matters to outsiders is taboo. Twenty-one per cent of the husbands voiced a complaint that their wives talked too much about personal matters to outsiders. The husbands were distressed to realize that their finances or marital conflicts were exposed to public view. Fewer men than women have confidants; only 7 per cent of the women have a similar grievance. The absence of the norm of friendship created certain psychological pressures to seek confidants outside of marriage. But this, in turn, resulted in violation of marital privacy.

Again, the Glenton ideal of masculinity with its emphasis upon emotional reserve and its identification of personal interchange with the feminine role resulted in what we have termed a "trained incapacity to share." . . . . Thus, even when a couple was exposed to the ideal of the companionate marriage, this lack of interpersonal competence occasionally hindered its realization. Indeed, the intellectual acceptance of such an ideal aroused in some couples feel-

[6] For the effect of mobility upon marriage see Elizabeth Bott, 1957; John M. Mogey, 1956; and Michael Young and Peter Willmott, 1957.

[7] Department of Labor release published in *The New York Times,* September 20, 1963.

ings of inadequacy. They knew that husbands and wives should talk to one another, but they found nothing to say. One measure of this problem is conveyed by two sets of figures. In response to one test story, 56 per cent of the wives held that something was lacking in the marriage of the couple in the story who had so little to talk about in the evenings. But as many as 44 per cent of the women, in another connection, complained that they frequently had nothing interesting to talk about with their husbands. For the husbands, the corresponding figures were 45 per cent, referring to the story, and 28 per cent, expressing a personal complaint.

The difficulties that hinder fuller realization of the ideal of companionship illustrate a familiar mode of social disorganization. Socially structured obstacles stand in the way of attaining the newly emerging cultural goal.[8] With respect to marital communication, our data enabled us to compare the magnitude of this discrepancy between aspirations and attainment for men and women at each educational level. The older high school women experience the widest gap between their expectations, on the one hand, and the actual quality of the marriage dialogue, on the other. They are consequently more dissatisfied with marriage communication than the less-educated wives at the same stage of life, despite the fact that they actually enjoy a higher level of sharing and companionate interchange.

The reader may argue that the personal dissatisfactions described above do not constitute social disorganization. Granted that the families continue to function without the social supports or restraints required by more seriously disorganized groups. Nevertheless, since the function of companionship is an increasingly important raison d'être of marriage, marital unhappiness by definition implies the failure of this social system to attain one of its goals, with unfavorable consequences for the fulfillment of other goals, including that of child-rearing.

The function of companionship has been frequently cited by sociologists as the distinctive feature of modern marriage. Many

[8] See Robert K. Merton, 1957, pp. 162–164.

writers have described the evolution of the modern family with specialization in its functions.[9] The remaining functions have been variously described as affectional or expressive and child-rearing or socialization. "We have argued above," concludes one recent discussion, "that the nuclear family is specialized far over in the expressive tension-management and socialization directions."[10]

If Glenton families are at all typical of comparable classes in other communities, then for considerable segments of our population these writings are more prescriptive than descriptive. They define the appropriate functions of marriage in modern society. But the logic of the analysis does not unfortunately bring the required patterns into existence automatically. Possibly even for the unhappy third of the Glenton couples, marriage entails some satisfactions. But these men and women do not turn to one another for emotional support, and it is uncertain whether the net effect of the marriage relationship is to relieve or to increase personal tension.

Let us recapitulate our analysis. Modern marriage is called upon to fulfill new functions of friendship and emotional support, partly as a result of mobility and isolation of the couple and partly in response to new cultural expectations stimulated by the changing status of women and other trends. The fulfillment of these functions is impaired in Glenton by the persistence of some traditional values and definitions of sex roles. These operate directly in sanctioning certain behavior and indirectly, through their detrimental effects upon interpersonal competence. The relatively low educational level of Glenton respondents plays, no doubt, an independent role in retarding the development of skills and attitudes required for psychological intimacy between the sexes.

The survival of dysfunctional values and attitudes is not the only source of social disorganization in Glenton. Were the residents themselves asked to rank their difficulties, the economic situation would head the list. Their relatively low occupational and educa-

[9] William F. Ogburn, Robert M. MacIver, Ernest W. Burgess, Harvey J. Locke, and Talcott Parsons, among others.

[10] Talcott Parsons and Robert Bales, 1955, pp. 162–163.

tional resources create a wide gulf between desired goals and attainments. . . . Not only the poorest fourth of the families, but others also live from one pay envelope to the next, with no savings or insurance to cushion a possible crisis. This explains the undercurrent of anxiety which repeatedly comes to the surface in such remarks as, "He worked good last year. I hope he will this year," or "I hope we'll stay healthy." Public relief is too humiliating to contemplate for these people, and in moments of panic they are much more likely to think of their relatives as a possible source of assistance.

For the man, the economic difficulties have a special emotional significance—they undermine his self-esteem. For example, he is concerned about his parental responsibilities. Our question, "Would you like your son to follow in your line of work?" was generally answered negatively, "No, I would like him to do a lot better." But at the same time the fathers doubted their ability to provide for their children the necessary means of advancement.

The husbands experience some other characteristic strains. Their actual power in the family frequently falls short of their patriarchal aspirations. In contrast, successful professional husbands may occasionally enjoy more power in marriage than is sanctioned by their egalitarian ideals.[11] The twinges of guilt which this latter discrepancy produces are less painful than the workingman's problem. Our respondents thought that "men should have the final say-so in family decisions." However, they found themselves pitted against resourceful wives who held paid jobs prior to marriage and could hold their own in marriage. This is especially true of the women high school graduates. One young wife told the interviewer that her husband's current weekly wages were only $10.00 higher than her own pay before marriage. Even the good providers lack the halo of prestige which high achievement and high community status bestow on a successful business or professional man. . . .

The lack of occupational and educational skills hinders the

[11] See Peter Pineo, 1961, for a discussion of a middle-class sample. . . . [A] similar observation about class differences in patterns of strain has been made by William J. Goode, 1963, p. 21.

attainment of desired goals but this does not drive Glenton residents to resort to illegitimate means. Several possible explanations suggest themselves for the low rate of deviancy. In comparison with lower socio-economic groups, especially those with racial and ethnic disadvantages, these native born Protestants may feel less alienated from society and more strongly committed to its moral codes and legitimations. We have already noted, for example, that their individualistic ideology made Glenton's poor providers deflect the blame for their low achievement from social conditions to personal failings. Moreover, the majority of Glenton's families have not given up the hope of improving their own economic position within the blue-collar class. By projecting their ambition to move out of the working class onto their children they feel that they remain true to the American norm of striving.

The relatively poor adaptation to the economic environment is, of course, a familiar theme in the literature on the working classes. Less familiar is the effect upon marriage of the poor utilization of the cultural, recreational and social resources of the community, also associated with this class position. The drabness of life puts a heavy burden upon the marriage relationship. Shortening of the work day, smaller families, and the withdrawal of many economic functions from the home have given these couples long evenings and weekends together. But life in general is impoverished, and marriage assumes a saliency by default. It is questionable whether any relationship can fill so great a void. Even the middle-class suburbanite, who has reputedly forsaken the world for the family nest, bristles with outside interests in comparison with our respondents. Status seeking, the elaboration of living standards, the social life, to say nothing of civic and cultural interests, fill life with tension and struggle but also with emotional involvement and rewards. The romantic ideal which decrees that each find in his mate the fulfillment of all his needs is, after all, only rarely attainable. Many marriages remain satisfying precisely because each partner can draw upon other sources of stimulation, amusement, response and accomplishment. These rewarding experiences may be shared in marriage thus nourishing the relationship. They may also compensate for whatever frustrations may be entailed in marriage. Of course, outside interests occasionally become so all-absorbing as to divest marriage of any emotional significance or they may violate the limits of cultural permissiveness as in the case of extra-marital sex. But given some psychic congeniality, the richness of life enjoyed apart from the marital relationship per se may sustain the latter and make it not merely tolerable but rewarding.

As for Glenton couples, those in their twenties still enjoy social life and other forms of recreation. The birth of children and the striving to purchase a home and to furnish it still give life a sense of movement. But many couples in their late thirties, especially among the less-educated, seem almost to have withdrawn from life. There they sit in front of the television set: "What's there to say? We both see it." "If you had two extra hours every day, how would you like to spend them?" asked the interviewer, and a man mused: "This would make the evening awfully long and tiring if you're watching T.V."

The social isolation, especially of the older men, has been repeatedly noted. We have described the relatively low involvement of the men, as compared with their wives, in the lives of their married children. Social life with friends also declines with age. Only infrequently do the men appear to enjoy emotionally significant ties with work-mates. They lack even the kind of segmented, though intense, relationships that business and professional men frequently have with co-workers.[12] If this social isolation is characteristic of working-class men of other ethnic, religious, and regional groups, it may play a role in explaining the relatively lower level of mental health in blue-collar strata as compared with the middle and upper classes.[13] In any event, this social isolation, we believe, tends to strain

[12] See Robert Dubin, 1956, for a research finding to the effect that "only ten per cent of the . . . (surveyed) workers perceived their important primary social relationships as taking place at work." For a comparative study of a professional group, see Louis H. Orzack, 1959.
[13] Thomas S. Langner and S. T. Michael, 1963.

the marriage relationship. It robs life, and therefore marriage, of stimulation and novelty and it closes outlets that might siphon off marital irritations.

We were slow to perceive the problem brought about by a drab existence and constant "togetherness," for a reason that illustrates anew how tacitly held values can distort perception. We approached the study with the image of the East London working-class marriage in mind. Will the American working-class marriage, we asked, show the same estrangement between the sexes? Do husbands and wives in Glenton, as in London, lead their separate lives in work and in leisure? The English pattern fell short of our own ideal of friendship in marriage.

Glenton families were found to differ significantly from the East London ones. Most wives know to the penny what their husbands earn, and economic decisions are made jointly. There is no lack of togetherness in the sense of time spent in each other's physical presence. Indeed, these couples probably spend more time together as a family (and probably more time together as a pair, without children, relatives, or friends) than middle-class couples with their more active social and club life. Our own moral set led us to approve these deviations from the East London patterns, and we were temporarily blinded to the problem that togetherness entailed for our respondents. We mistakenly assumed that the greater association between the spouses automatically brought about a deeper relationship than in East London.

Not all of Glenton families experience the difficulties just enumerated with equal intensity. The high school graduates on the whole are happier in marriage than the less-educated. . . . This is especially true in the first years of marriage. The better-educated marry later and delay child-bearing in comparison with the less-educated couples. Consequently, fewer of the former suffer from the syndrome of problems of some young couples: too many infants, parenthood too soon after marriage under difficult economic conditions and in the absence of companionship between the mates. Moreover, the high school men (perhaps because they are younger), do not include the completely defeated men whose sense of failure has such unhappy consequences for marriage.

While high school graduates also believe in the traditional division of labor between the sexes, in practice the husbands help more frequently with the care of infants and with shopping than in less-educated families. Equally significant is their fuller marital communication. They have more faith in the possibility of friendship between men and women. One young high school graduate explained why women have more need of heart-to-heart talk than men: "The husband's job is an outlet for him and her days are more routine and so she needs to sit down and feel the closeness with her husband." When depressed, this wife finds that "a good heart-to-heart talk can do a lot for her morale." A value endorsed so explicitly must surely affect behavior. In contrast, the less-educated tend to feel . . . that friendship is more likely to exist between persons of the same sex and that the principal marital ties are sexual union, mutual devotion and complementary tasks.

But the better-educated have some typical problems of their own. Status frustration is one of them. Generally, status-seeking is not a prominent drive among these families. There is an order of priorities in goals and many are preoccupied with sheer survival. Even the more prosperous families do not live with gazes fixed on their reflected image, and with the constant comparative self-appraisal allegedly so characteristic of our society. This is no "other-directed" group. Many a middle-class couple who have to cultivate the "right" people for the sake of the husband's career would envy the freedom these families enjoy to entertain only the people they like. Their social life, such as it is, is pure sociability. Nevertheless, some pressures for upward mobility do exist and some high school couples exhibit strain because their aspirations for higher status are frustrated. . . .

We found no difference between the two educational groups in the prevalence of sexual problems or in psychological sources of marital strains. No personality tests were employed in this study, and observations about psychological factors in marital maladjustment here appear inconclusive. But some speculation is aroused by the higher proportion of hostile sons and daughters among the less-educated couples, caused apparently by a number of social factors in their early lives. An unhappy childhood and hostile parent-child re-relationships tend to affect adversely the marital adjustment of the individual.[14] If this excess of parent-child conflict among the less-educated is confirmed by future studies it will offer another possible explanation of their lower marital happiness.

We limited our summary to problems in marriage, brought about, directly or indirectly, by socio-economic and cultural conditions. But there is hardly a case history . . . which does not suggest psychological factors involved in marital strain. Sharing a home with in-laws need not necessarily create an in-law problem, but it requires, as we have seen, a closer emotional dove-tailing of personalities if trouble is to be avoided. Given the same degree of congeniality, those residing in separate households will experience less strain. Given a common residence, variations in psychological factors will also produce variations in the outcome. . . . Maintaining the fiction of her husband's supremacy in public is, for example, an accepted stratagem of a dominant wife. But this adaptation to a deviant situation is not available to some personalities. We encountered a wife whose competitiveness with her husband, more or less dormant in the privacy of the home, is aroused by the presence of an audience.

The summary of Glenton's problems was further limited to those most likely to be class-linked. The book itself illustrated many other sources of social disorganization: discontinuities in sex roles throughout the life cycle; ethical inconsistencies consequent upon social mobility and social change, yielding unearned advantages to either husbands or wives; situational pressures giving rise to operative norms which occasionally violate the ideal code and others. Among social sources of psychological stress, our case studies revealed an interesting variety. It is well known that culture may cause stress by censuring some desired gratification or by mandating a goal difficult to attain. But social factors may affect the degree of

[14] Clifford Kirkpatrick, 1963, pp. 385–386.

stress also by making it more or less difficult for individuals to mask socially condemned motives. For example, the new social acceptance of working wives has not modified the husband's jealousy, his anxiety over the possible loss of power and other personal objections to his wife's employment. Lacking the support of public condemnation, he is robbed of acceptable rationalizations in arguing his case and must expose, to himself and to others, his "irrational" objections. Again, the well-to-do wife, whose real motive for working is the wish for power, can hardly claim that she needs to contribute to family support. The Glenton working wives, on the other hand, could plausibly rationalize less acceptable incentives in economic terms.[15]

This study did not include any middle- or upper-class respondents, and it contains no data on broad class differences in marital adjustment. Recent evidence shows that divorce rates tend to decrease with higher socio-economic and educational status. The data on marital satisfaction are consistent; satisfaction appears to go up with the rise in the class hierarchy.[16] We have no information about the rates of divorce or desertion among the general population of Glenton's Protestant blue-collar families from which we drew our respondents. Nevertheless, our comparison of the two educational categories of blue-collar families has some pertinence to the question of broad class differences in marital happiness.

Current analyses of this problem seek to ascertain the peculiarly stressful experiences of the working classes in comparison with the upper strata.[17] But it is not certain whether the extent of stress does in fact decline as one ascends the occupational or the educational

[15] These observations suggest a new dimension to the factor of visibility in social relations. In the past it was the visibility of norms and of role-performance that was the object of discussion. Added to this now is the probability that social factors may determine the degree to which an occupant of some status can succeed in masking his motivations, or conversely, be forced to expose them.

[16] See bibliographies in William M. Kephart, 1961, and in William J. Goode, 1956 and 1963.

[17] See, for example, William J. Goode, 1956, p. 67.

ladder. The economic and occupational frustrations were indeed more prevalent among our less-educated respondents as they are, no doubt, in a comparable stratum in the society at large. But offsetting these and other difficulties of these workers is their freedom from a number of allegedly typical problems of the higher and better-educated classes. Ambiguous definitions of mutual rights and duties and the resulting ethical inconsistencies, mental conflict produced by an abundance of choices, conflicting loyalties and standards, strain produced by the sheer volume of stimuli—all these are relatively rare in Glenton. Glenton couples are also free from the self-conscious scrutiny of relationships that, some writers claim, robs marriage of its spontaneity among many highly educated persons.

Are we to assume then, ex post facto, that these problems, more prevalent among the higher classes, are somehow less disturbing than those typical of the workingman? [18]

The interpretation of this problem may require a shift in emphasis. It is an open question whether life is less stressful for the higher classes. But it must surely contain richer rewards.[19] The sense of satisfaction with marriage, as with life in general, may depend not so much upon an absence of stress as upon the presence of rewards—a momentary feeling of closeness with one's mate, the occasional excitement of hope, even a fleeting triumph of achievement. True, a low level of expectations inflates the rewards of minor attainments ("I had myself a ball once when I came out two dollars over the budget that we didn't have to pay out all at once"). But even with their modest aspirations, too many Glenton couples find life drab and unrewarding.

The paradox that higher socio-economic classes may experience both more happiness and more tension in marriage is no mere conjecture. The more highly-educated respondents in one study

[18] It is possible that the Glenton sample is too stable to be typical of working-class strata that are generally included in the class comparisons of marital adjustment. But the insulation from intellectual currents of the larger society and absence of group affiliations have been demonstrated in numerous working-class studies in other communities.

[19] See Alex Inkeles, 1960.

rated their marital happiness higher than people of less education; at the same time they expressed more self-doubt and a greater sense of inadequacy.[20] Further confirmation is supplied by a recent investigation which reveals that "high marital tension or job dissatisfaction may not necessarily produce unhappiness if they are offset by a sufficient number of positive feelings."[21] The better educated, higher income groups in the same study were found to exhibit a higher level of both positive and negative feelings. The authors conclude that "men of higher socio-economic status have a higher degree of marital tension, but at the same time happier marriages . . . [than men of the lower status]."[22]

Not only is the marriage relationship of the educated middle classes—in comparison with blue-collar workers—likely to contain more positive experiences, but so does their life in general. The more abundant life provides, as noted earlier, safety valves to siphon off marital frustrations and compensations to offset them.

Life at its best is economically comfortable and rewarding, but for the great majority life is narrowly circumscribed. A spotlight outlines a small circle of ground around each family, with the relatives, a few friends, the boss and some work-mates, the tavern keeper, the church and the union. Visible also are the top movie stars, baseball players and other athletes, T.V. performers and top national office holders. But beyond that circle extends a vast darkness. These English-speaking, well-dressed, well-mannered, responsible persons do not enjoy full membership in their society. They lack even such bridges to the larger society as may be provided by membership in a women's club or a Chamber of Commerce. The union occasionally (but from what could be ascertained, only infrequently) provides such a channel of information and sense of participation.[23] Verbal and intellectual limitations curtail reflection even about the immediate environment. In the

[20] Gerald Gurin, *et al.*, 1960, p. 116.

[21] Norman M. Bradburn and David Caplovitz, 1965, p. 39.

[22] *Ibid.*, p. 41.

[23] For a similar view see Joel Seidman, "The Labor Union as an Organization" in Arthur Kornhauser, *et al.*, 1954.

words of Beatie, the working-class rebel of *Roots:* "Ever since it began the world's bin growin' hasn't it? Things have happened, things have bin discovered, people have bin thinking and improving and inventing but what do we know about it all?"[24] Economically poorer racial and ethnic minorities are no doubt still more deprived, but this does not make the exclusion of Glenton families any less wasteful and disturbing.

This is not merely the judgment of the author. In considerable measure, this is also the respondents' self-appraisal. Why, otherwise, would a father exclaim with such feeling: "No, I want my children to go a lot farther." But for all their fervent hopes and the struggle, these parents cannot provide for their children the environment enjoyed by the average middle-class child. Unless school and society find ways to improve the life chances for all citizens, a proportion of Glenton's children will grow up to live as do their parents, on the fringes of their society.

. . . . .

SOME GENERALIZATIONS RECONSIDERED

A large proportion of current generalizations about marriage owe their derivation to studies of college graduates. Are such generalizations "universals" for our society? It will be particularly instructive to review some negative instances. The comparative perspective of this study brought to light the hidden assumptions and, therefore, the limited scope of some familiar generalizations.

Studies of in-law problems made in this country show these to be predominantly "women's problems." . . . This can be plausibly explained by the greater social involvement of women with relatives, by their greater sensitivity and jealousy and other psychological sex differences. But we found that the less-educated husbands experience in-law problems as frequently as do their wives. . . . Should future

[24] Arnold Wesker, 1959, pp. 74–75.

studies confirm this fact, the original generalization about the excessive feminine proclivity to in-law conflict in our society will have to be restricted to a particular social context.

Waller and Hill's idea that "the secrets of marriage are among its most important assets" appears plausible enough.[25] The secrets of marriage both express the solidarity of the pair and, in turn, weld it more strongly. Conversely, revealing marital dissatisfactions to outsiders would naturally appear to weaken the marriage. But . . . we argue that a number of the "low" blue-collar marriages are not harmed but actually made more viable because the partners—especially the wife—find emotional support in intimate relationships with friends and relatives. Not only was this support lacking in marriage; more significantly, neither mate expected to find it in marriage. The original generalization then holds only for marriage characterized by certain norms.

The recognition that marital interaction changes with the stages of the family cycle has led to the interest in the patterning of these changes. Many writers stress the disenchantment that sets in with the years of marriage. We cited, however, several indications that the curves of satisfaction differed for the two educational groups. Dissatisfaction with marital communication, for example, was actually higher on the part of the younger less-educated men than among those married seven years and over. The unfavorable circumstances plaguing some less-educated couples dispelled very soon the euphoria of early marriage. This raises the possibility that the typical curve of marital happiness throughout the family cycle may not be identical in various socio-economic classes. Moreover, the curves of satisfaction may vary from one aspect of marriage to another.

Several studies have reported a correlation between the sexual adjustment of a couple and their happiness in marriage. Our interviews suggest that the size of this correlation may vary with class. Because some of our less-educated women expect little psychological intimacy in marriage, and their standards of personal

[25] Willard Waller and Reuben Hill, 1951, p. 326.

relationships are not demanding, they were able to dissociate the sexual response from the total relationship. The sole high school graduate who was sexually fulfilled despite marital unhappiness appeared to have a masochistic personality.

The perennial debate about the causes of sex differences lends interest to comparative studies. That the social environment can affect emotional sex differences was demonstrated anew by our findings on empathy, the sources of emotional relief, on-admission of "being hurt," and other traits. Women were found to excel men in empathy only among the less-educated couples; with high school education differences between the sexes became smaller. But a constant residue of difference remains: women of both levels of education express a greater yearning for interaction with their husbands than vice versa. Is this a true "universal" for our society? In one study, college-educated men cited "lack of closeness between husband and wife" as a marital problem more frequently than did college-educated women.[26]

Different class backgrounds of the spouses have been found to be unfavorable to marital adjustment.[27] However, we encountered cases in which intermarriage promoted adjustment. For example, one husband who married "down" found that his wife, brought up in a patriarchal milieu, granted him more privileges than he had been conditioned to expect. He was appreciative of her generosity. His wife's lower social background did not interfere with his semi-skilled job as it might have had he been a junior executive in a corporation. Although no doubt they are more often unfavorable, the effects of intermarriage vary with the significance of the particular differences between the spouses in the social context of a given marriage.[28]

One of the more interesting recent developments is the application to the family of theories derived from the study of small

[26] Orville G. Brim, Jr., *et al.*, 1961, p. 224.

[27] Ernest W. Burgess and Leonard S. Cottrell, Jr., 1939.

[28] See Anselm L. Strauss, 1954, for a study of American-Japanese intermarriages.

groups. The positive relationship between the extent of talking and dominance in decision-making, noted in small groups, has been confirmed by Fred L. Strodtbeck in experimental sessions with married couples.[29] We did not study this problem systematically, but in several of our cases the dominant partner was the less talkative of the two; these may of course have been exceptions to the general pattern. But one can readily see that in a group of strangers a silent person can hardly make his influence count. In marriage, however, we deal not only with a smaller group but an enduring one. Over the years of marriage a person can exert his influence in other ways than through sheer volume of words. "He doesn't say much but he means what he says and the children mind him," a mother says about the father. The same may apply to the couple's marital relationship.

Sidney M. Jourard and Murray J. Landsman found a high degree of reciprocity in self-disclosure in a study of friendship.[30] Our married couples present a similar picture but in a number of marriages one partner is considerably more reserved than the other. Here again the differences between the family and other small groups may account for the divergence. Lack of reciprocity may tend to make friendship less rewarding to the participants and therefore unstable. Marriage, on the other hand, is held by many ties. The more independent, or the more withdrawn, partner may reveal less of himself than his mate without thereby endangering the stability of marriage.[31]

Other generalizations have been modified by the findings of this study. Among the questions raised at the outset of this inquiry were some involving dilemmas of choice. Will work or the family claim the major emotional commitment on the part of the workingman? Does he find his greatest rewards in personal relationship or in achievement? Will our respondents spend relatively

[29] Fred L. Strodtbeck, 1951.

[30] Sidney M. Jourard and Murray J. Landsman, 1959–1960.

[31] For some differences between the family and other small groups see Fred L. Strodtbeck, 1954, and Talcott Parsons and Robert Bales, 1955, pp. 303–306.

more of their leisure together or with individual hobbies? Will the conjugal or the parental family claim the primary loyalty? Will domesticity or the job bring the greater gratification to the working wife? We assumed the existence of these dilemmas because time and energy are limited. Moreover, some of these goals are not only competing but conflicting since the means which further one, hinder the other.

But we soon realized that this formula, "The more of one, the less of the other," often does not fit the facts. The workingman neither brings home a briefcase nor spends the evening in social life with friends. He is absorbed neither in his career nor in hobbies. Our high school graduates tend to be both more intent on achievement than the less-educated and more emotionally involved in marriage. The better-educated women enjoy more joint leisure-time activities with their husbands, but also spend more evenings in club work and with girl friends away from home.

Is the day, we began to wonder, equally long for all social classes? The answer is that it is not, that the less-educated have a less abundant life all around because neither time nor energy is fully used.

The assumption that all have an identical volume of energy and time was not our sole fallacy. Certain attitudes tend to be considered antithetical because of fortuitous historical circumstances. There may have been a time when only women who rejected domesticity would crave an outside job. But we encountered women who had an exceptionally favorable attitude to both domesticity and work, and others who found few satisfactions in either.

Some sets of values have the sound of a logical antithesis but in fact tend to be associated. The high school women reveal more of themselves to their husbands than the less-educated wives. But they also appear to have a greater respect for privacy. When we asked one high school graduate not to discuss the study with her husband prior to our meeting with him, she voiced a value in her reply: "This was *my* interview and I don't have to share it with him." She was happily married and her communication was rated "very full." Her high standard of personal relationships included both the value of sharing and respect for privacy. A person embracing both values may sometimes experience a conflict between them. But in comparing two groups, we find that one of the same group tends to endorse both. Similarly it is probable that a complex person has an acute need both for occasional privacy and for self-revelation.[32]

To sum up, most generalizations concerning American marriages have been based predominantly upon studies of middle-class and educated respondents. . . . [M]any of these propositions withstood the test of this investigation. Others proved to be class-linked. The study of blue-collar marriages brought to light the hidden premises of several familiar generalizations and has thereby enabled us to reformulate them with greater precision.

REFERENCES

BOTT, ELIZABETH, "Urban Families, Conjugal Roles and Social Networks," *Human Relations,* 8 (1955), 345–384.

BRADBURN, NORMAN M., and DAVID CAPLOVITZ, *Reports on Happiness,* Chicago: Aldine Publishing, 1965.

BRIM, ORVILLE G., JR., *et al.,* "Relations Between Family Problems," *Marriage and Family Living,* 23 (August 1961), 219–226.

BURGESS, ERNEST W., and LEONARD S. COTTRELL, JR., *Predicting Success and Failure in Marriage,* New York: Prentice-Hall, 1939.

DUBIN, ROBERT, "Industrial Workers' Worlds," *Social Problems,* 3 (January 1956), 131–142.

GOODE, WILLIAM J., *After Divorce,* Glencoe, Ill.: Free Press, 1956.

——, *World Revolution and Family Patterns,* Glencoe, Ill.: Free Press, 1963; London: Collier-Macmillan, 1963.

GURIN, GERALD, JOSEPH VEROFF and SHEILA FELD, *Americans View Their Mental Health,* New York: Basic Books, 1960.

INKELES, ALEX, "Industrial Man: The Relation of Status to Experi-

32 See an interesting discussion of dilemmas of family living in Clifford Kirkpatrick, 1963, pp. 90–95.

ence, Perception and Value," *American Journal of Sociology,* 66 (July 1960), 1–32.

JOURARD, SIDNEY M., and MURRAY J. LANDSMAN, "Cognition, Cathexis, and the 'Dyadic Effect' in Self-disclosing Behavior," *Merrill-Palmer Quarterly of Behavior and Development,* 6 (1959–1960), 178–186.

KEPHART, WILLIAM M., *The Family, Society and the Individual,* Boston: Houghton Mifflin, 1961, p. 618.

KIRKPATRICK, CLIFFORD, *The Family as Process and Institution,* New York: Ronald Press, 1963.

KORNHAUSER, ARTHUR, ROBERT DUBIN and A. ROSS, eds., *Industrial Conflict,* New York: McGraw-Hill, 1954.

LANGNER, THOMAS S., and S. T. MICHAEL, *Life Stress and Mental Health,* New York: Free Press of Glencoe, 1963.

MERTON, ROBERT K., *Social Theory and Social Structure,* Glencoe, Ill.: Free Press, 1957, pp. 161–195.

———, and ROBERT A. NISBET, *Contemporary Social Problems,* New York: Harcourt, Brace, and World, 1961.

MOGEY, JOHN M., *Family and Neighborhood, Two Studies in Oxford,* London: Oxford University Press, 1956.

ORZACK, LOUIS H., "Work as a 'Central Life Interest' of Professionals," *Social Problems,* 7 (Fall 1959), 125–132.

PARSONS, TALCOTT, and ROBERT BALES, *Family Socialization and Interaction Process,* Glencoe, Ill.: Free Press, 1955.

PINEO, PETER C., "Disenchantment in the Later Years of Marriage," *Marriage and Family Living,* 23 (February 1961), 3–11.

ROTH, JULIUS, and ROBERT F. PECK, "Social Class and Social Mobility Factors Related to Marital Adjustment," *American Sociological Review,* 16 (August 1951), 478–487.

STRAUSS, ANSELM L., "Strain and Harmony in American-Japanese War-Bride Marriages," *Marriage and Family Living,* 16 (May 1954), 99–106.

STRODTBECK, FRED L., "Husband-Wife Interaction over Revealed Differences," *American Sociological Review,* 16 (August 1951), 468–473.

———, "The Family as a Three Person Group," *American Sociological Review,* 19 (February 1954), 23–29.

WALLER, WILLARD, and REUBEN HILL, *The Family,* New York: Dryden Press, 1951.

WESKER, ARNOLD, *Roots,* Baltimore: Penguin Books, 1959, pp. 74–75.

YOUNG, MICHAEL, and PETER WILLMOTT, *Family and Kinship in East London,* Glencoe, Ill.: Free Press, 1957.

SELECTED BIBLIOGRAPHY

BURCHINAL, LEE G., "Research on Young Marriages: Implications for Family Life Education." *Family Life Coordinator* (September, 1960), pp. 6–24.

COHEN, ALBERT K., and HODGES, HAROLD M., JR., "Characteristics of the Lower-Blue-Collar Class." *Social Problems* (Spring, 1963), pp. 303–34.

KANIN, EUGENE J., "Premarital Sex Adjustments, Social Class and Associated Behaviors." *Marriage and Family Living* (August, 1960), pp. 258–62.

KOHN, MELVIN L., "Social Class and Exercise of Parental Authority." *American Sociological Review* (June, 1959), pp. 352–66.

RAINWATER, LEE, *And the Poor Get Children.* Chicago: Quadrangle Books, 1960.

VINCENT, CLARK, *Unmarried Mothers.* New York: Free Press of Glencoe, 1961.

WARNER, LLOYD W., MEEKER, MARCHIA, and EELLS, KENNETH, *Social Class in America.* New York: Harper & Row, Publishers, 1960.

FAMILY DESIGN: MARITAL SEXUALITY, FAMILY SIZE AND CONTRACEPTION

Lee Rainwater

In cultures around the world, marital sex usually has been considered important for two purposes—for reproduction and for satisfying the sexual needs of the husband. While women could and did receive personal satisfaction from sexual relations, it was not usually an expected right. In the patriarchal societies of the past, sexual need often was assumed to be a need of only the man. The woman who also received sexual satisfaction was sometimes viewed by her husband (and herself) as somewhat "unnatural." "Good" women did not usually derive pleasure from the sexual act. Their role as sexual partner was relegated to that of duty to the husband. With few effective methods of controlling conception, the result of marital coitus was frequently pregnancy. This often resulted in

Source: Pp. 277–300 of FAMILY DESIGN: MARITAL SEXUALITY, FAMILY SIZE AND CONTRACEPTION by Lee Rainwater. First published 1965 by Aldine Publishing Company. Reprinted by permission.

a large number of children, a high maternal mortality rate, and a short life span for the reproductive wife.

In the American middle class of today, the traditional patriarchal beliefs about marital coitus have been altered. No longer is conception viewed as beyond the control of the individual. Through the development and use of birth-control methods, conception is becoming increasingly controllable. Another change in the traditional beliefs is that the wife now has as much right to expect sexual fulfillment in marriage as has her husband. In effect, then, the two general social changes concerning marital coitus have had their greatest impact on women.

However, many of the middle-class values concerning marriage generally and sexual relationships particularly are either absent or modified in the lower class. When there is a husband present, lower-class marriages tend to be patriarchal. Often this may be the case only in assuming his rights of authority and not in assuming his obligations. Sharing—which is characteristic of middle-class marriage—is often absent in the lower class. Men and women of the lower class do have some knowledge of sexual intercourse and are generally aware that methods exist for controlling pregnancy, but this knowledge is limited. In an earlier study, Rainwater found that both husbands and wives consider sexual gratification for the wife much less important than for the husband. The wives generally seem content when intercourse results in the husbands' pleasure and not in their own. As long as the husband obtains sexual satisfaction, the wife feels that continuing to have the sex "weapon" in dealing with him is adequate compensation for her own lack of sexual satisfaction. As a result, marital sex may be seen as a constant battle, with the male "getting" but trying not to give and the wife "giving" and hoping to get something else in return.

The following selection is taken from the concluding chapter of Rainwater's book. In this study, he relates the respondents' views concerning sexuality and control of family size. His study is important because most other studies of family planning in the

past have paid little or no attention to either values or behavior patterns of marital sex. The participants in the study were selected according to the major variables of class, race, and religion. This study reports on a total of 409 people, including both husbands and wives, although not all were married to each other. The technique used was an open, conversational type of interview.

This study traces out in detail one major subcultural variable, that of social class, and deals also with one other extremely important variable, religion, as a control variable. The reader will have noted that there are many cases [in] which Catholics and non-Catholics within a given social class do not differ, just as there are many in which they do. Further, social class is seen as exercising its influence primarily through two characteristics of the family as a social system which vary from one class subculture to the other: first, the conjugal role-organization, values, and practices that are characteristic of different social classes, and second, the particular role concepts and the values and practices attendant on them that are deemed appropriate for men and women in different social classes. The first category has to do particularly with the kind of separateness and connectedness, the division of labor, that is characteristic of marital relations; the second has to do with the various nonfamilial role behaviors that are to be expected of men and women.

Any study that proceeds past the demographic level of analysis (in which variations by socio-economic status are demonstrated) must make use of some set of intervening variables such as these, since class per se does not influence behavior of any kind. It is only the culture and social system within each class subgroup which differentially influences behavior. The intervening variables, then, provide something of the "why" for the demographic facts of variation by social class groups. The influence of social class subcultures conceived in this way is traced out here in connection first with sexual relations in marriage, then with family size preferences and motives, and finally with respect to family limitation behavior in terms both of types of methods used and relative success with each method.

ROLE-ORGANIZATION

A high degree of conjugal role segregation is found most commonly in the lower class, with intermediate degrees of segregation in the upper-lower and lower-middle class and an emphasis on joint role-organization in the upper-middle class. Along with this go typical concepts of how the husband and wife act in their roles. In the higher status groups there is heavy emphasis on outside activities, on involvements that can be viewed as bringing resources into the family (intellectual and artistic interests, social activity, etc.). This emphasis is relatively infrequent at the lower-middle class level and still less frequent at the upper-lower class level. Emphasis on outside activity, at least by the husband, is apparent at the lower class level but here these activities are viewed as potentially dangerous to the family, either from waste of income or because they are regarded as precursors of indiscretion by the husband.

All of this adds up to a strong emphasis in the middle class, and also among those of the upper-lower class who participate in the pattern of intermediate segregation, on the resolution of family difficulties by discussion, compromise and mutual accommodation. In contrast, relatively few lower class husbands and wives use such techniques. They accommodate instead to a pattern of a high degree of segregation and often to a pattern in which there is a good deal of dissatisfaction with the marriage on the part of both partners.

SEXUAL RELATIONS IN MARRIAGE

We have tried to examine here some aspects of patterns of sexual gratification in marriage. Our goal has had to be modest because this was only one of many subjects in which we were interested and also because we were dealing with an area that can be probed only superficially unless a particular kind of rapport is developed in which the respondent becomes motivated to search his own feelings and memory with frankness and accuracy. (Kinsey and his collaborators seemed to achieve this rapport, although unfortunately they used their opportunity more to count than to understand.) However, given the relative paucity of non-clinical information on sexual relationships in marriage, we believe our data have considerable value and allow for a somewhat more dynamic understanding of marital sexuality than previous studies permit.

Respondents were given an opportunity to express their feelings about their sexual relationship in response to several different kinds of questions and they were encouraged to speak as freely and in as much detail as they wished. From the open-ended material which resulted, assessments were made of the level of sexual gratification that respondents seem to find in their marital relationship or at least to seek in it; also, certain specific attitudes and views about the relationship were noted. From this analysis it appears that the degree of sexual gratification varies quite markedly by social class, and in the lower class also by type of conjugal role-organization. Both men and women, but particularly women, more frequently find gratification in sexual relations in the middle class than in the lower class, and within the lower class, in relationships characterized by less segregated role-organizations. It also becomes apparent that in the less segregated relationships the husbands are more likely to know how their wives feel about sexual relationship, whether they find sex gratifying or not. Going along with this, wives in highly segregated relationships are much more likely to think of their husbands as inconsiderate of their feelings in connection with sex than are others.

Similarly, there is greater emphasis on purely "physical" gratifications in the lower class and among highly segregated couples and more emphasis on social-emotional gratifications in the middle class and among less segregated couples. There is some evidence that within the middle class the highest degree of interest in and value placed on sexual relationships occurs in families where there is also a high degree of emphasis on togetherness and a family-centered focus of activities. The more individualistically oriented upper-middle class couples seem much more concerned about placing sex "in perspective" with other meaningful activities.

FAMILY SIZE—PREFERENCES, NORMS AND MOTIVES

Studies of ideal family size conducted over the past twenty-five years document an increasing focus on a moderate ideal of two to four children. As Ronald Freedman (1962) notes, the important question for research on family size becomes whether or not we can "explain the variations within this range by reference to a combination of social and psychological variables." While from the broad macroscopic focus of the demographer the concentration of over 90 per cent of choices for ideal family in the two-to-four-child range suggests a homogeneity of preference, the differentiation within that range suggests to the family sociologist important questions for research.[1]

[1] As a methodological aside, it should be noted that the common practice of presenting family size data in the form of averages ("3.2 children") tends to obscure the fact that we are dealing with a very short scale of three numbers. For most purposes it probably makes more sense to treat this as a set of qualitative categories than as a continuous range. For example, to specify the increase in ideal size as from 3.0 in 1941 to 3.4 in 1955 obscures the fact that during that time the proportion of persons preferring four children doubled, the proportion preferring two children was halved, and the proportion preferring three children changed not at all. While an average takes less space on a page, this economy is hardly sufficient compensation for the relative paucity of information it carries. This is not simply a methodological issue. When one examines the way couples talk about the different sizes of families, one becomes aware that psychologically this is not a continuous distribution but a highly discontinuous one.

In our sample there is a tendency for middle class Protestants and Catholics to offer smaller ideal family sizes than their lower class co-religionists; while there is some tendency for these same differentials to apply to the number of children the couples themselves want, the tendency is not nearly so strong. When people are asked whether they believe that there is a trend toward larger or smaller families, the reverse obtains. That is, middle class people tend to see a trend toward larger families while lower class people see a trend toward smaller families. This suggests that a good many lower class people are saying that what they want are small families within the range they believe to have been common in their group, while for middle class people, the ideal numbers are those that represent relatively larger families within the range they believe to have been characteristic of their group. The lower class respondents are suggesting greater prudence in the ideals they offer while the middle class respondents are suggesting greater affluence.

When one examines the rationales offered by respondents for large and small families it is possible to abstract one central norm about family size: *one should not have more children than one can support, but one should have as many children as one can afford*. "Afford" is the operative term here, and men and women recognize that families vary in the number of children they can truly afford. While there is no hard and fast norm in our society which says that we should have two or three or four children, this should not be taken to mean that in this situation sanctions are not exercised by significant others or that internalized sanctions are not significant. Rather, the way people talk about their own family size and the family sizes of others suggests clearly that the thinking of husbands and wives about the number of children they should have is strongly influenced (albeit selectively) by normative considerations they have internalized as participants in the larger society.

Thus, there seems to be general agreement that to have fewer children than one can afford is an expression of selfishness, ill health, or neurotic weakness; to have more is an expression of poor judgment or lack of discipline. Implicit in the comments of the great majority of respondents is the idea that when people are able to have a large family, they want a large family. The good person does this. The person with moral failings stops short of the number he can afford in order to have something extra for himself or for his fewer children, and these extras connote selfishness in the parent and cause it in the child. The child gains from being a member of a larger family by being less spoiled, less selfish, more co-operative in giving, and he has more fun. The parent of a larger family gains from a greater chance to love and be loved, and he lives in a happier milieu. The "stingy" parent instead, lives with his small family according to a life plan that emphasizes goods for himself and his children, time and freedom for outside interests, and education.

Having a larger family, then, becomes a way of resisting materialism, a way of spreading the wealth and thus avoiding some of the evils people believe inhere in materialistic self-indulgence. Affording a given size of family is therefore only superficially conceptualized as an economic matter. Nonetheless, this is the most acceptable reason for not having more children, and people believe it is the major legitimate factor behind variations in preferred family size. Parents vary in the extent to which they perceive the question of "affording" in terms of short-term or long-term economic issues, the major long-term concern being that of the cost of educating children. It is interesting that there is not a larger class variation in this as a rationale for smaller families; the knowledge that the demand for educated workers is increasing seems very widespread, and at each class level the necessity for children staying in school longer tends to be picked up by people as an important rationale for desiring a smaller family.

A central problem for any given couple in arriving at an optimum family size is that of selfishness versus responsibility. It is interesting that having a large family is often described as a manifestation of irresponsibility. There is implicit here the notion that larger families can be very enjoyable but this is an enjoyment one cannot afford. However, less clearly verbalized than relatively straightforward financial concern are concerns about the psychic costs of having a large family. These tend to be poorly formulated; to admit that one could not handle a larger family tends to be taken as an admission of weakness, and to want only two children for this reason is thought to represent a kind of psychosocial hypochondriasis. There seems to be little clearly formulated conception of what children might gain in non-financial ways from growing up in a smaller family. It is the parents who gain in this area by having greater freedom to pursue their own interests, and this is in sharp contrast to the belief that both parents and children gain from the luxury of interpersonal pleasures and growth in a large family.

There seems to be a fairly widespread pattern of active discussion of family size, both in general and specifically in terms of one's own needs and desires. Only a small minority of those in our sample deny ever having discussed family size with anyone. The kinds of people with whom family size is discussed vary by social class; in somewhat simplified form, the following pattern emerges: At the lowest status level, the wife's mother and sometimes other females in her family form the core of those concerned with how many children the couple has, and the subject is casually discussed with relatively few others. At higher status levels, the members of the husband's family become more involved, and also friends outside the family are more often included in these discussions. Thus considerations of family size are interpersonally more complexly conditioned at higher than at lower status levels. Although the data in this study contain only very tentative leads to this process of interpersonal influence on testing and evaluating decisions concerning family size, the kinds of comments and justifications people offer for their own particular decisions suggest strongly that decisions about family size are not immune to the influence of both the extended family and the peer group.

We can make much more sense out of the functions of large and small families for middle class couples than we can for lower class couples because the former are more likely actually to have the number of the children they desire and no more. Thus, it is possible to compare with some confidence the manifest reasons these couples offer for their preferences, and to probe some of the deeper motivations involved by comparing these groups in terms of certain background social psychological characteristics. From the previous discussion of rationales offered for different family sizes, it should not come as a surprise that middle class couples who prefer larger families tend to be those who indicate a greater need to deny selfishness and to validate and symbolize their identity as larger and more moral persons. These people tend to see most clearly the interpersonal gains they can offer their children by providing them with a larger family and also to perceive for themselves the gains of enhanced self-esteem that come from thus denying themselves in order to be good parents. This is particularly true of men; the more manifest level of the functions of small and large families do not seem to differentiate the family size preferences of middle class women.

The functions of a small family are also more obvious at the manifest level for men than for women. Middle class men who want a smaller family seem to find gratification in thereby confirming their identities as sensible persons, as men who understand well the long-range interests of their children. At the same time, middle class men who want smaller families do not seem really to have much understanding of why other men might want larger families. In general, both men and women who want smaller families seem less involved with the whole question of family size; they are less likely to discuss questions of family size widely with others, either relatives or friends. Perhaps they feel somewhat out of step with the rest of the society, and try to minimize the divergence between their own minority views and those of the larger middle class world in which they live.

At the deeper level of motives, our data provide some support for the hypotheses outlined by Hoffman and Wyatt (1960) concerning factors which differentiate couples preferring large and small families. The first of these hypotheses states that larger families are functional for resolving housewives' conflict over whether or not, and how, to be active in the world outside the home, either through a job or through other kinds of outside activities. Women who seek and find gratifying outside activities which are not anxiety producing tend to prefer smaller families, and those who do not find such activities tend to prefer larger ones. Conversely, women who find their homemaking responsibilities demanding and/or providing opportunities for creativity will tend to prefer smaller families. The second hypothesis has to do with the parent role. Here Hoffman and Wyatt note that an emphasis on the parent role can function to make up for a sense of lack of involvement in the homemaking role; activity as a parent can make up for the declining creativity that is provided by the homemaker role as housekeeping becomes more mechanized and prepackaged. By increasing the number of children they have, couples can feel they have an opportunity to practice both more fully and for a longer period of time a set of interpersonal skills which have become highly valued in our increasingly child-centered society. The anxiety which tends to accompany parental functioning may also tend to encourage larger families, since parents will seek to assuage their guilt over not doing a good job by having more children and hopefully doing a better job with the younger ones. Also, involvement with the very demanding routine of young children may serve to distract and to justify difficulties parents have in measuring up to their ideals of parental care and guidance for their older children.

We have seen that parents who want large families tend to emphasize the gains that children have by virtue of their contact with other children. Thus it would seem that one way of coping with the increased emphasis on good child-rearing practices is to see in the large family a child rearing gain per se; that is, to emphasize that each additional child contributes to the socialization of the others by helping to create an atmosphere that at once builds character and makes for fewer demands on the parents (since the children can make demands on each other). The large family serves to moderate the intensity with which parents take their child-rearing responsibilities by spreading it over more individuals. Parents are able to verbalize their belief that having a large number of children both increases the individuality of each child and brings about a desirable lower emotional involvement of the parent in the individual child.

The data in our study which seem to provide a test of these related hypotheses are of several kinds. First, we find that, as one would predict from the Hoffman-Wyatt hypothesis, middle class wives who describe themselves primarily in terms of their orientation to outside social and intellectual interests, or to their husbands as companions, tend overwhelmingly to prefer a small family, whereas those who describe themselves solely as orientated to their children tend overwhelmingly to prefer large families. Those who emphasize both outside and home orientations most frequently prefer medium families and next most frequently, large families. (This cannot be accounted for simply by differences in family size at the time of the interview.) Similarly, one could hypothesize that in the families in which there is emphasis on joint role-organization the wife will tend not to orient herself to a large family, whereas in those characterized by a relationship of intermediate segregation the wife will tend to look to her children for a sense of deeper interpersonal involvement. This holds true in our data: wives who are in relationships of intermediate segregation overwhelmingly prefer larger families, and those in joint relationships tend to prefer small or medium sized families.

The Hoffman and Wyatt hypothesis suggests that women who are particularly concerned with their responsibilities as homemakers and parents will tend to prefer smaller families, whereas those women who are particularly concerned about their possible self-definition as egocentric or selfish will tend on a compensatory basis to prefer large families. In our data, a majority of those who think of their main "bad point" as involving an inability to stand up to the pressures of their roles (too nervous, anxious, depressed, or unenergetic) overwhelmingly prefer small or medium sized families, whereas those who think of their main bad points as involving egocentricity, selfishness, and stubbornness tend to prefer larger families. The fact that the majority are concerned with an inability to measure up to the demands of their family roles suggests that one should not overemphasize the extent to which wives feel that their homemaking functions do not fully involve them.

Third, Hoffman and Wyatt hypothesize that as more and more individuals in modern society are characterized by aloneness and alienation, one compensatory mechanism adopted by couples has been that of having larger families, thus providing themselves with a ready made primary group to which husband and wife can retreat for meaningful interpersonal relating. We have less relevant data here. While our data clearly indicate that Americans see the family as offering these possibilities, we are not able to test in any systematic way the extent to which those husbands and wives who prefer large families are particularly characterized by a tendency to be alienated. That is, we can say that compensation for alienation is a function which larger families serve for those who have them, but we cannot say that this is a differential motivation for desiring larger families. It may simply be a secondary gain.

Further, we can hypothesize a kind of curvilinear influence of alienation on fertility preferences. It would seem equally reasonable to believe that to the extent to which individuals become sharply alienated from the representations of value in their society, as they feel more isolated and cut off from a meaningful identity with the collectivity of which they are a part, they will be less interested in having children (indeed, perhaps less interested in marriage). As persons become more isolated, one would expect that they would also become more narcissistic and self-involved and less willing to cope with demanding interpersonal relationships. Perhaps the relationship between alienation and family size desires is curvilinear, in that individuals who are highly alienated will not want to become responsible for large families nor will individuals who are deeply integrated into a large network of significance. On the other hand, individuals who feel threatened by a tendency toward aloneness and alienation, but who are still hopeful about the possibilities of avoiding the pain of that state, may seek to do so by creating a meaningful primary group with a larger number of children. One finding in our data seems to bear on this point. We find that among a majority of couples for whom sexual relations are not very important to either partner, at least one partner wants a small family, whereas an overwhelming proportion of couples for whom sexual relations are very important to both partners want a medium sized or large family. We take this as confirmatory of the hypothesis about extreme alienation, since we believe that highly alienated individuals will not be able to establish marital sexual relations in which both partners attach a great deal of importance to these relations.

CONTRACEPTION AND FAMILY LIMITATION

We have discussed contraceptive behavior in terms of generalized attitudes toward the possibility of planning a family, the discussions husband and wife have of this subject, the kinds of methods known and used and the effectiveness with which they are used, and finally, the attitudes which couples express toward different kinds of medical and family planning clinic approaches to contraceptive advice and prescription.

Several different approaches to the whole question of how one might plan a family and limit the number of children one has were evident in our data. Some couples approach this subject in a very planful and taken-for-granted way. They are interested in the technical aspects of contraception. They expect to be able to plan their families and they feel that they have developed routines that make it possible for them to do so. Other couples are hopeful on this score, but uncertain. They are not sure that what they are doing will work and their general attitude is one of involved and optimistic uncertainty—somewhat like the feelings the typical suburbanite often has about his lawn. Finally, there is an attitude that can be summarized as fatalistic—an attitude of relatively low optimism, a sense of (at most) going through the motions of family planning with a rather low confidence that one's abilities will suffice to achieve the desired goal and a tendency, therefore, not to be particularly involved in the mechanisms of family planning. The first attitude, the planful one, seems by far the most common among middle class couples, particularly Protestants, and much less common among lower class couples, particularly those at the very bottom level. Whatever their particular knowledge of contraceptive methods or the strength of their personal desires to limit family size, couples at the lowest class level seem to show relatively little confidence that they will be able to make successful use of the methods known to them.

These patterns of attitude toward family planning, in general, tend to go along with particular patterns of husband–wife discussion of contraception and family limitation. By and large, there was full discussion early in marriage among middle class Protestants. This was somewhat less characteristic of middle class Catholics, who tended to have only casual discussion of the subject, particularly since they expected to have large families and did not think it necessary to concern themselves with the problem of family planning and limitation until fairly far along in their child-bearing history. At this later phase, however, most middle class Catholics did begin to discuss family planning fully and seriously and to bring this subject more centrally into their marital planning. Within the lower class there was a strong tendency among Protestants and Catholics, Negroes and whites alike, to postpone full discussion of this as a marital task until fairly late in the couple's life together. It was much more common among lower-lower class couples not to discuss the subject more than casually, even after having had more children than either partner wished. As other researchers have noted . . . the resources for communication and co-operative decision-making in lower class families are often not up to the task of making and carrying out sensible decisions about contraception even when there is a desire for family limitation on the part of both partners.

Our data indicate a widespread knowledge of the existence of different contraceptive methods among all groups in the sample.

Only among lower-lower class Catholic women are there more than 4 per cent of the respondents who are not able to name at least one contraceptive method. Although the number of methods of which individuals are aware varies rather markedly by social class, with middle class people able to name more methods than lower class people, it also seems clear that even at the lower class level there exists the knowledge of one or two methods which have the capacity of limiting conceptions. At the simplest level of knowledge, then, even lower-lower class couples seem at least as well equipped as were the higher status persons in Europe and England at the time these latter groups began limiting their families. One or the other of the two medically approved methods of choice, the condom or the diaphragm, come readily to mind for over 80 per cent of the men and women in each of the subgroups in our sample.

It would be difficult to maintain, then, that anyone in our sample does not effectively limit his family because of lack of knowledge, if knowledge is construed in a purely intellectual sense. If to this is added a social dimension (knowledge that a method exists that other people use routinely and effectively, and in which, therefore, one may [place] some confidence) or a psychological dimension (knowledge that the method which one knows to exist is emotionally acceptable and is in one's means to manipulate successfully), then the matter appears in a very different light. Construed in this way, however, "knowledge" is hardly different from motivation and conviction about a method's appropriateness, and rational elements take a decided back seat to more emotional and interpersonal factors.

It is in this sense that people seem to assess their own knowledge when asked how much they knew about contraception when they were married and how much they have learned since. Middle class women are more likely to assess their knowledge as adequate at marriage and to feel that they have learned a good deal since, so that now they know a great deal more about contraception and family limitation than they need to know. The same is true of middle class men. In sharp contrast, lower class women very often assess their knowledge of contraception at marriage as low and they tend to feel that they are only modestly well-informed even at present. There is a strong tendency on the part of lower-lower class respondents to assess their knowledge of methods as something by itself, as not integrated either into their own sense of available technology or into their worlds. They know about methods but do not understand them, they seem to be saying. Their lack of understanding is not simply technical; it extends to the whole social process of planning a family with contraceptive methods. Upper-lower class men and women do not say they started marriage much better informed than men and women in the lower-lower class, but they feel they have learned more, even when this means only that they have learned a sense of *really* knowing something about the same methods whose names they knew earlier in marriage. The main thing they seem to have learned is to accept contraceptive methods as part of their world and to seek to master the technology that is involved.

Knowledge of contraceptive methods in the middle class, particularly among Protestants, seems to be pursued not only in terms of direct functions for the couple but also as a matter of interest. Thus middle class men and women are much more likely to learn about new methods that come on the market, even though they do not immediately adopt them. They seem also to be oriented toward trying to select the "best" method from among those available, rather than simply settling on an acceptable method. Thus, women who for many years have used and apparently been satisfied with the diaphragm shift to oral pills as they begin to get the idea that this is now the best method.

Middle and lower class people differ in the ways they think about the effectiveness of family planning. Middle class people tend to have high confidence in some methods (condom, diaphragm, pills) and to have a low expectation of method failure. They seem to believe that most people have accidents either because they are too ignorant to use effective methods or because they do not use effective methods correctly. In other words, middle class people tend to differentiate methods rather sharply in terms of effectiveness and to differentiate users in terms of competence. In the lower class these distinctions are very much blurred. There is a greater tendency to see the more effective methods as subject to failure, and also a greater tendency to see the less effective ones as perhaps proving adequate "if you're lucky." There is a similar tendency not to see competence in using contraceptive methods as paying off, but rather to feel that one is always at the mercy of the method's inherent shortcomings. Thus lower class people are much more likely to blame the method, much less likely to blame the user. This is particularly true of the lower-lower class.

Within the lower class the choice of methods seems to some extent determined by the kind of conjugal role-relationship the couple has. Those in joint or intermediate relationships are much more likely to choose one of the effective feminine methods (diaphragm, pill, cream, or jelly alone) and those in highly segregated relationships are more likely to use one of the "folk methods" (douche, withdrawal, rhythm incorrectly understood). Approximately equal proportions of the two groups use the condom. Several factors seem to operate here. Couples in less segregated relationships are more confident about the success of family planning and therefore more likely to use an effective method. The choice of a feminine method (principally diaphragm) needs a good deal of support from the husband if the wife is to feel secure about what she is doing, and such support is available only to the wife in the less segregated relationship. She needs support to cope with the fears that she often has about the diaphragm and its mysterious functioning.

EFFECTIVE CONTRACEPTIVE PRACTICE

The couples in our sample were categorized as either effective or ineffective contraceptive practitioners on the basis of their descriptions of the methods they used and the ways they used them. While this is a rough categorization, it does represent the typical practice of couples in the sample as they were able to report it to us. The reader should understand that some of the effective practitioners may on occasion "take a chance" but do not report this to us, instead indicating that they try to be regular about their use of a method. Ineffective practitioners on the other hand either use methods in ways that minimize their effectiveness (as with many of the lower class rhythm users), use no method at all, or indicate that their use of effective methods is sporadic. Overall, about half of the ineffectives in our sample use no method and the other half use a method but not in such a way that it is likely to prove effective. The latter is much more true of the lower class respondents in our sample; the former is primarily true of the middle class and of Catholics in all classes. Ineffective practice varies quite strikingly by social class, both before and after the birth of the last wanted child. In the latter case, 98 per cent of middle and upper-lower class Protestants are classified as effective as are 73 per cent of the comparable Catholics. At the other extreme only 13 per cent of lower-lower class Catholics and Negroes and 33 per cent of lower-lower class Protestants are classified as effectives. Among those who finally do become effective contraceptive practitioners, there are systematic variations as to timing, with 96 per cent of the middle class becoming effective before the birth of the last wanted child and 44 per cent of lower-lower class Catholics and Negroes becoming effective only after the birth of an unwanted child.

We hypothesized that effective practice would be positively related to lesser segregation in the conjugal role-relationship, and this proves to be true, both before and after the birth of the last wanted child but particularly in the latter case. We take this relationship to indicate the importance of communication between the husband and wife and involvement by the husband in family issues. In the more segregated relationships it is much more common for the husband to regard the whole question of family planning as mainly his wife's business. While most of Stycos' (1962) argument about the shortcomings of the feminist and medical biases of traditional Planned Parenthood and Public Health approaches to family planning is convincing and solidly based in available evidence, his argument at times seems to substitute an equally unreasonable masculine bias. It seems likely that there are many areas of the world in which lower class subcultures are characterized by a low operating commitment by the husband to what goes on in his household, whatever formal norms of masculine-dominance may obtain. It would seem most useful to encourage family planning workers to tailor their approach to the particular patterns of conjugal role definition that exist in the groups they seek to serve, rather than to encourage on a blanket basis either a feminine or masculine emphasis.

We find also a positive relationship between effectiveness at contraception and the extent to which the wife indicates that she finds sexual relations with her husband gratifying. This relationship does not hold for Catholics but only for lower class white Protestants and Negroes. The relationship between sexual gratification and contraceptive effectiveness is a complex one and seems also related to the nature of the conjugal role-relationship. A highly segregated conjugal relationship makes it difficult for couples to function in the close co-operation required both for mutually gratifying sexual relations and effective contraceptive practice. In this context, contraception tends to become a bone of contention in relation to the wife's wish to avoid anything connected with sex, and her aversion to sexual relations is reinforced by her anxiety about becoming pregnant coupled with the difficulties she experiences in doing anything effective to prevent it.

Correlations with effective and ineffective contraceptive practice within the middle class are not easy to come by. First of all, both before and after the birth of the last wanted child, well over 90 per cent of the middle class Protestant couples were effective practitioners. This is not to say that these people may not have accidental pregnancies, but our method was not sufficiently refined to investigate accidents as opposed to the generalized habit of ineffective contraceptive practice. It would be interesting to study the kinds of couples who have accidents, particularly ones which result in more children than one or both partners wanted. A minority of middle class Catholics do continue ineffective contraceptive practice past the birth of the last wanted child, but we have not been able to determine what the difference is between those Catholics who do this and those who instead become regular practitioners of an effective method (including rhythm).

However, while the major variable of importance within the lower class—the conjugal role-relationship—does not seem to be related in the middle class to effective versus ineffective contraceptive practice, a variable concerning the sexual relationship of a couple is related to effective practice before the birth of the last wanted child for both Catholics and Protestants. Among couples in which husband and wife indicate equal levels of enjoyment of the sexual relationship, almost 90 per cent of the couples were also effective contraceptive practitioners, whereas among those couples in which one partner enjoyed sexual relations more than his spouse only about half of the couples were effective contraceptors. It seems possible that in relationships of unequal enjoyment there is a tension which repercusses on contraceptive practice, either by affecting the kind of method which is acceptable to the couple, or by affecting the regularity of use. The latter seems the stronger possibility since the relationship holds for both Catholics and Protestants and therefore across a number of methods, including most particularly diaphragm, condom, and rhythm. It is also possible, of course, that among couples who find anxiety in their sexual relationship rather than security and comfort there may be a tendency to delay effective contraception in the unconscious hope that additional children will improve the relationship. Thus, there would be less emphasis on family planning and spacing of children through effective contraception.

MEDICAL ASSISTANCE FOR FAMILY LIMITATION

For the greater part of history, family limitation and contraception have been only partly under the control of medicine. It is only in the past thirty or forty years that many couples have turned to physicians as the primary source for learning about contraceptive methods. With the development of the diaphragm, chemical methods of contraception, and lately the pill, the expertise of the physician has come to seem necessary if one is to have the most effective method available. We were interested, then, to see to what extent couples of different classes had availed themselves of medical counsel in connection with contraception. Almost all of the middle class Protestants had done so, but a third, or slightly more, of all the other groups had never discussed contraception with a physician. The use of Ob-Gyn specialists was concentrated in the middle class. Lower class whites were much more likely to use a general physician when they sought such advice, and lower-lower class Negroes were relatively more likely to receive such advice post-partum in a hospital. Within the lower class, Negroes in the upper-lower class were most likely to use Ob-Gyn specialists. Planned Parenthood was most often used by Negroes, perhaps as a function of the location of clinics in Chicago where the majority of Negroes in the sample lived. The availability of medical counsel does not seem by itself strongly related to effectiveness of contraception practice, a finding which is not surprising considering that the condom is well known and available to anyone who wants to use it.

Among lower class whites the type of medical contact does not seem related to whether or not a couple is effective or ineffective. But among lower-lower class Negroes there is much more likelihood that effectives have sought out advice on an out-patient basis or gone to Planned Parenthood; ineffectives are much more likely to have been the more passive recipients of advice when the wife is in the hospital after the birth of a child. Our results suggest that this kind of post-partum advice, at least as it is given to Negroes in Cook County Hospital, has not been particularly useful. When lower class women discuss the medical contacts they have had with respect to contraception, it is obvious that the physician has a difficult problem with which to deal. The hurried advice that these lower-lower class Negro women say they received in the hospitals often was not sufficient to enable them to go further in adopting an effective method.

Since one or another kind of more assertive program for making contraception available to couples seems necessary, we sought to tap attitudes toward three different kinds of assertive family planning programs: (1) a greater assertiveness on the part of physicians in bringing up the subject with their women patients, (2) Planned Parenthood clinics, and (3) door-to-door family planning programs. In general the response to all three programs was quite positive. Middle and lower class, Protestant and Catholic, men and women seemed to be more favorably disposed toward medical assertiveness in this area than one might have thought.

Protestants almost unanimously agree that the physician should volunteer advice to his patients about family planning and limitation. This applies across class lines, but seems to be particularly important for lower class patients who more often indicate that they are too embarrassed to bring up the subject themselves and wish the physician would. In the lower class, Catholics do not differ from Protestants in their positive attitudes on this score, but among middle class Catholics views are more varied; almost all acknowledge that where the wife's health is involved the physician has a responsibility to discuss family limitation with her, and a substantial minority takes a more secular attitude and says that he should bring the subject up for whatever reasons he feels are adequate.

Most respondents indicate a positive but rather distant attitude toward the value of Planned Parenthood clinics. Middle class Protestants think they are a very good idea, but of course, not for them, since they have their own physicians. A few middle class Catholics expressed strong hostility toward the idea of Planned Parenthood, and a similar number endorse the idea of the clinics heartily. The majority of Catholics indicate a conditional acceptance of the idea based on the notion that someone should help poor people plan their families, usually saying that such clinics are all right for people who have no religious objections to the idea of family limitation.

Within the lower class there are, then, very favorable attitudes toward the idea of Planned Parenthood clinics. Yet we know that few of the respondents have ever used these clinics. The particular conception that these lower class respondents have of the clinic seems to mitigate against their using them more fully. The most general formulation of these attitudes is that these people believe the organization is mainly for special problem cases, and they are reluctant to define themselves in this way. They believe that Planned Parenthood is for the very, very poor, or for those with very large families, or for people who are too ignorant to be able to figure things out on their own. The woman who has these feelings is reluctant to define herself in this way by going to the clinic.

Responses to the idea of a door-to-door family planning program were considerably more positive than had been expected. Middle class people generally thought that such a program would be useful since they believe that there are many women who need to limit their families and want to, but do not know how to do so. The responses on this score closely parallel those for attitudes toward Planned Parenthood except that, surprisingly, middle class Catholics are more often favorably disposed to the idea of a door-to-door program than they are to Planned Parenthood clinics. Apparently they feel more comfortable about a program which does not carry the "controversial" Planned Parenthood name. Lower class respondents indicate few misgivings about the door-to-door approach as prying or an invasion of privacy. Instead they suggest that women would feel more comfortable all the way around about learning about family planning in their homes rather than in the alien atmosphere of a clinic. We are not, of course, evaluating the effectiveness of a door-to-door program here; but our data do suggest that there would be little direct rejection of family planning workers who go into the community to seek clients.

SELECTED BIBLIOGRAPHY

BRODSKY, STANLEY L., "Self-Acceptance in Pregnant Women." *Marriage and Family Living* (November, 1963), pp. 483–84.

CHRISTENSEN, HAROLD T., "A Cross-Cultural Comparison of Attitudes toward Marital Infidelity." *International Journal of Comparative Sociology* (September, 1962), pp. 124–37.

FREEDMAN, RONALD, WHELPTON, PASCAL K., and CAMPBELL, ARTHUR A., *Family Planning, Sterility and Population Growth*. New York: McGraw-Hill Book Company, 1959.

GUTTMACHER, ALAN F., *et al., The Complete Book of Birth Control.* New York: Ballantine Books, Inc., 1961.

KINSEY, ALFRED C., POMEROY, WARDELL B., MARTIN, CLYDE E., and GEBHARD, PAUL H., *Sexual Behavior in the Human Female.* Philadelphia: W. B. Saunders Co., 1953.

MASTERS, WILLIAM H., and JOHNSON, VIRGINIA E., *Human Sexual Response*. Boston: Little, Brown & Co., 1966.

OGG, ELIZABETH, *A New Chapter in Family Planning*. New York: Public Affairs Committee, Inc., 1964.

POFFENBERGER, SHIRLEY, POFFENBERGER, THOMAS, and LANDIS, JUDSON T., "Intent Toward Conception and the Pregnancy Experience." *American Sociological Review* (October, 1952), pp. 616–20.

WESTOFF, CHARLES F., POTTER, ROBERT G., SAGI, PHILIP C., and MISHLER, ELLIOT G., *Family Growth in Metropolitan America*. Princeton, N.J.: Princeton University Press, 1961.

WINCHESTER, A. M., *Heredity and Your Life*. New York: Dover Publications, Inc., 1960.

THE CHANGING AMERICAN PARENT

Daniel R. Miller and Guy E. Swanson

In the past, beliefs about the rearing of children have generally had a strong parental orientation. That is, parents usually reared their children according to their own needs and values as parents. But in the United States, a transition in childrearing has been made from parental to child orientation. The changes in childrearing and child care have been so extensive in the American middle class that there may be significant differences in beliefs from one generation to another. Childrearing procedures in recent years have undergone such rapid change that mothers sometimes feel concern not over whether what they are doing is right, but whether it is still "believed" to be right. One can almost select childrearing beliefs at random and then, by looking around, find some experts to support them.

In the United States, the modern, urban middle-class family is no longer bound together by the traditional family ties. Without the

---

Source: Pp. 215–33 of THE CHANGING AMERICAN PARENT by Daniel R. Miller and Guy E. Swanson.

strong kinship supports and without the related dependency of women on men, new kinds of family ties have had to be developed. These new ties center around the ego-needs of the family members; but the needs themselves are influenced by social values from outside the family. In the following selection, Miller and Swanson suggest that the middle-class family of today is becoming increasingly bureaucratic, because the society stresses bureaucratic values and the family feels compelled to prepare its children to move into that social setting. In rearing its children, the middle-class family is faced with the problem of teaching the children to be competitive enough to stand out to some degree, but not to be so different they will be viewed as threatening to generally accepted values. In the "bureaucratic" middle-class family, the child interacts with his peers as colleagues whose favor he must seek out and whose respect he must win. In a society where being liked is important, the child is often taught not to select one or two close friends and ignore the others, but to learn to fit in smoothly with all of his age peers.

Today's parents seek to restrict their children's behavior to a more limited set of standards than did the parents of the past. The parents may want the child to learn the rudiments of playing the piano, but they will not want him to be a pianist. The child should be bright but not brilliant, attractive but not beautiful, and a good student but not an outstanding one.

To determine some of the patterns of and beliefs about child-rearing, Miller and Swanson conducted interviews with 582 mothers having one or more children under nineteen years of age living in the household. The interviews were done in 1953 using a "three-stage area sampling" procedure, selected from among all the census tracts in the Detroit Metropolitan Area. It is that feature—the large and carefully selected sample—that makes this study outstanding. In the chapter that follows, the authors present some findings about child care along with an overview of child training based on what they found from their sample.

With this chapter we come to an ending and a beginning. Here we give the last of our findings about child care. But here we also take a first step to permit a more adequate study of changes in methods of training children.

From time to time we have wished that information comparable to that which we now possess were available for urban America of fifty or a hundred years ago. With such information we could make clear and firm judgments on many questions about which we now can only speculate. And—what is equally important—we would not be forced to use the existing older middle classes as representative of an older style of life. We know they are already touched in important ways by the new styles of living and hence are "impure" examples of their kind. For many purposes, a superior way to study change is to take periodic samples from the stream of history.

What we can do is to make a first investment in providing the materials for later and longitudinal research on changes in child care. We can present the findings from our study in such a way that they may provide benchmarks against which future investigators can match their own results. For this future purpose, we shall no longer separate mothers by race, social class, or any other basis, but shall report how all our Detroit mothers, taken together, answered our questions. We will present a composite snapshot of Detroit's families in the early spring of 1953. Where existing information permits, we shall try to illumine the picture of Detroit mothers by comparing it with information collected from the study of child training in other societies.

We have arranged our findings about the methods of rearing children to correspond roughly to the sequence with which mothers introduce each of these methods. For this reason we begin with expectations about having a new baby. Then we review the ways in which eating, sucking, and defecating are socialized. Following this, we report findings on methods of discipline and on demands that the child act responsibly. The guidance of sex-related behavior is then discussed. Finally, we present our material on the mothers' expectations about the adult roles their children will play. The number of cases for which responses are reported is 582 when the questionnaire item was administered to all mothers. It is 291 when the item was administered to only a random half of the mothers. . . .

THE NEW BABY

In the judgment of our coders, based on the mothers' answers to Items 1, *1a,* and *1b,* the infancy of 66 per cent of Detroit's children represented very pleasant experiences to their mothers. Another 18.6 per cent of the mothers were rated as finding a new baby mildly pleasant. Almost 14 per cent were rated as finding him unpleasant.[1] Although we have no data from outside the United States with which to compare these ratings, we find it a striking possibility that more than one out of every ten mothers finds the arrival of a new baby more depriving than rewarding.

The attitudes of mothers affect babies through their appearance in specific maternal behaviors. We turn, therefore, to our findings concerning such matters as the feeding of infants, the control of their defecation, the provision of discipline, and training the growing child to be independent.

FEEDING

The body regimens of infancy have had much attention in our earlier chapters. There are times when writers in the popular women's magazines speak as if the whole of the child's personality were set by the age of weaning or whether he was breast-fed. Our immediate concern is not with such problems, but with what mothers do.

[1] The percentage not ascertained is 1.9.

About 41 per cent of the children in our study were fed solely on the bottle, only 10 per cent were fed solely at the breast.[2] A common pattern was that of the 40.1 per cent of the cases in which the mother began by suckling the child at the breast and later switched to bottle feeding. In 7.4 per cent of the cases the child was bottle- and breast-fed from the beginning.[3]

Another popular theme in the writings about child rearing is the importance of demand or scheduled feeding. We find that almost 57 per cent of the children studied were on demand feeding and about 41 per cent on scheduled feeding. We were unable to get information about these matters in 2.3 per cent of the cases.[4]

Of those children who were fed only by bottle, and for whom weaning was completed, 63 per cent were weaned completely by the end of the twelfth month, 90 per cent by the end of the eighteenth month, 99 per cent by the end of the twenty-fourth month, and 1 per cent at later times.[5] The proportions for those who were breast-fed at some time are almost identical.

These findings on age of weaning are one of the few pieces of information for which we can make some fairly accurate comparisons with the practices of a large number of other societies. There are, of course, countless fragments of information on other topics covered in our study, but the methods of gathering and recording the data are not usually comparable with the ones we have used. Weaning information, because it is expressed in terms of a specific number of years, is far more standardized from study to study. It also is a point which American and European anthropologists are likely to investigate among non-literate peoples since it often differs from our own practices.

Recently, Whiting and Child, an anthropologist and a psychologist, have published the results of cross-cultural investigation of child training and personality. It includes a summary of these weaning data for the largest number of societies ever examined for this

[2] See Items 4, 5, and 6.

[3] The percentage not ascertained is 2.7.

[4] See Items 5*e* and 6*c*.

[5] See Items 6*b*.

purpose.[6] They began their research by going through all the information in the Human Relations Area Files under the headings of Infancy and of Child Care.[7] These files represent a massive attempt to record all reputably known facts about all societies—more especially about all non-literate or primitive societies. The files are incomplete even with respect to existing knowledge, but they give the most comprehensive coverage now available for anyone who wants to make a large number of comparisons of life in a variety of societies. From these files the investigators uncovered considerable information about child-training practices in sixty-five societies. They also added data from ten other societies not yet incorporated into the files. All seventy-five societies are primitive.

From information thus gathered, Whiting and Child conclude that demand feeding is the pattern practiced by most people in all the societies they sampled. As indicated above, this is also true for our Detroit area mothers. We have the impression, however, that the percentage of Detroit mothers who feed babies on a schedule is higher than that to be found in any of the groups studied by Whiting and Child.[8]

Their second conclusion is that the typical society (among the fifty-two cases in their sample for which relevant information was available) is one in which weaning begins at thirty months.[9] We have two figures from Detroit. For infants who have had some breast feeding, the median age at which weaning is begun is nine months. For babies fed only on the bottle, the median age is eleven months. Whiting and Child report that the societies they studied range in this respect from those, like our own, which begin weaning before the end of the first year of life to those which wait until the

[6] John W. M. Whiting and Irvin L. Child, *Child Training and Personality, A Cross-Cultural Study* (New Haven: Yale University Press, 1953).

[7] For a more complete description of the nature, coverage, and uses of these files, see George P. Murdock, "Feasibility and Implementation of Comparative Community Research with Special Reference to the Human Relations Area Files," *American Sociological Review*, 15 (December, 1950), 713–720.

[8] Whiting and Child, *op. cit.*, 69. [9] *Ibid.*, 70–71.

fifth or sixth year. Less than 2 per cent of the mothers in our sample continued breast or bottle feeding beyond the child's second year. It is clear that mothers in the Detroit area wean their children far earlier than is typical in this group of primitive peoples. Unfortunately, we have no comparable material for other literate or urban and industrial societies against which to match our own.

For some time there has been a belief[10] that the newborn baby takes great pleasure in sucking parts of his body. Much conflicting evidence has since been gathered[11] on the problem of whether this pleasure is independent of joys of eating, as such, in puppies and rats and kittens and in human infants. It still is uncertain whether or not the very act of sucking is pleasurable to the human child as an inherent consequence of his biology.

It will be recalled that we asked if the children in our study ever sucked their thumbs, arms, hands, or "something like that."[12] About 34 per cent of the mothers said the child had. About 64 per cent said, "No."[13] We have already given our reasons for feeling that many of the negative answers to this question represent a distortion of the true facts. Because the truth of these negative answers is in doubt, we are more interested in the detailed answers of the parents who said "Yes." About half of them felt it necessary to do something to stop the child's body sucking. Two-thirds of these used mechanical or chemical preventives like finger covers or jaw braces or evil-tasting liquids. The others tried to divert the child or give him acceptable substitutes.[14]

10 See, for example: Sigmund Freud, *Three Contributions to the Theory of Sex* (A. A. Brill, trans., New York: Nervous and Mental Disease Publishing Co., 1920).

11 For a recent study of this topic and a bibliography of pertinent experiments, see: Theodore H. and Lili R. Blau, "The Sucking Reflex: The Effects of Long Feeding vs. Short Feeding on the Behavior of a Human Infant," *The Journal of Abnormal and Social Psychology,* 51 (July, 1955), 123–125.

12 See Item 2.

13 The answers of another 1.7 per cent were not ascertained.

14 Seventeen per cent of the mothers who said "Yes" did not tell the interviewer what methods they used.

DEFECATION

Of course there is some overlap in the periods of time involved in weaning and in the beginning of bowel and bladder disciplines, but, for convenience, we have separated our treatment of them. We found that 6.7 per cent of our mothers had not yet started bowel training.[15] Of the remainder, 57.6 per cent began between six and nine months, 84 per cent began by the end of the twelfth month, 97.7 per cent by the end of the eighteenth month, and only an additional 2.3 per cent during or after the nineteenth month. Complete bowel control, both day and night, was established by the end of twelve months in 26 per cent of the cases, between the thirteenth and eighteenth months in 36 per cent of the cases, between the nineteenth and twenty-fourth months for 22 per cent, and after the twenty-fourth month for the remaining 16 per cent.[16]

The pattern for beginning urinary training is similar. The relevant periods and proportions appear below:[17]

Months	*Percentage*
0—12	66.6
13—18	23.5
19 and above	9.9

The only appreciable difference is that urinary training seems to begin somewhat later than bowel training in the general population. The following are the data for the age at which, when the question applied, urinary control was completely attained:[18]

[15] See Item 14. Responses from 2.5 per cent of the sample were not ascertained.

[16] See Item 16. Some 3.9 per cent of the sample did not provide a response to this item. Another 9.2 per cent had not yet completed bowel training.

[17] See Item 17. The percentage of responses not ascertained is 5.6. Almost 12 per cent of the mothers had not yet completed urinary training.

[18] See Item 18. Urinary control was neither begun nor completed by 25.4 per cent of the respondents. Responses were not obtained from 3.9 per cent of them.

Age at which toilet training was begun, like age of weaning, is specific enough to enable some comparisons with the practices of other societies. In Whiting and Child's sample of primitive groups, information on this point was in the files for twenty-five societies.[19] Their cross-cultural tables are not quite comparable to ours since they do not distinguish between the start of bowel and urinary training. However, the results are still of interest since, for toilet training generally, Whiting and Child find the typical primitive society beginning this regimen at eighteen to thirty months. Our

Months	*Percentage*
0—12	24.0
13—18	22.0
19—24	25.0
25 and above	29.0

mothers start much earlier. They typically begin bowel training at eight to nine months and urinary training at eleven to twelve months. Whiting and Child report a range of times for beginning to teach defecation control running from one to five years. Only 2.1 per cent of our mothers began bowel training after a year and a half, and only 8.3 per cent of them started urinary training later than that age. Again it is evident that mothers in the Detroit area make demands for the socialization of body functions at an earlier date than do most primitives.

In the case of bowel training we also have some information about the way the parents handled the child who "didn't want to get on the toilet, or [who] was uncooperative and wanted to get off the toilet."[20] To begin with, 20.8 per cent of the mothers said they had had no such difficulties with their youngsters or that these difficulties lasted too short a time to be important. Some 3.9 per cent said they had such difficulties but did nothing about them, 24.4 per cent removed the child when he resisted, 18.7 per cent kept him on and tried to make the experience pleasant with diversions and en-

[19] Whiting and Child, *op. cit.,* 74.

[20] See Item 15.

couragement, and 19.4 per cent, while keeping him on the toilet, accompanied this with close supervision, spankings, or other stern measures.[21]

DISCIPLINE AND RESPONSIBILITY

The differences in disciplinary technique connected with toilet training are not restricted to this single situation. We presented our respondents with the case of a child of ten years who had done something with which the mother was extremely upset or angered and asked what she would do. The distribution of answers appeared like this: [22]

Punishment	*Percentage*
Stimulates guilt or shame	2.1
Scolds, threatens	25.1
Restricts behavior and withdraws privileges	44.2
Physical punishment	22.3
Would not punish	2.5
Do something; what, not ascertained	1.1

It seems that the general population of mothers is split into a group of only 22.3 per cent which spanks or slaps the child, one of just over 25 per cent which scolds and threatens, and a large proportion (44.2 per cent) which uses restriction of behavior (e.g., keeping in the house) and withdrawal of privileges (e.g., sending to bed early, cutting allowance). The choice often publicized in the newspapers between physical punishment and the absence of any punishment at all is hardly crucial for most of the population.

[21] The item was not applicable for 6.7 per cent of the mothers since they had not begun toilet training the child. In another 5.3 per cent of the cases, the response of the mother was not ascertained.

[22] About 1 per cent of the cases were those in which a response to this question was not ascertained.

In previous chapters we have also discussed symbolic and direct rewards. We have seen that the entrepreneurial and bureaucratic populations in Detroit do not differ in their use of these methods. How does the total population stand in this respect? A question, similar in generality to that for punishment and also involving a ten-year-old child, was asked concerning reward.[23] We got the following results:

Reward	*Percentage*
Psychic reward: satisfactions expected to come from within the child for a job well done	5.6
Other verbal praise	62.2
Special privileges or freedoms	5.6
Material reward: money, gifts, etc.	18.7
Demonstrations of love and affection	1.1
Some reward; what, not ascertained	0.7
No reward	3.2

And, what might be done by the child to deserve such punishments and such rewards? The examples our mothers gave are not hypothetical. The questions required them to think of their own child at age ten and to tell us what might have angered or pleased the parents a great deal. In their answers, then, we have some record of the problems and pleasures which children afford parents.[24] The lists are familiar to any parent. The child who is considered too daring or who shows signs of straying from parental supervision and rules—these are the common problems. In looking over the examples of good behavior we find little emphasis on virtue and altruism in a general way and much weight given to the performance of those acts that signify integration into the common life of the family, in the operation of the home, and in formal school preparation for the child's own future activities. These acts also outweigh the child's

[23] See Item 19. In some 2.9 per cent of the cases no response was ascertained for this item.

[24] See Items 19*a* and 20*a*.

Examples of Misbehavior	*Percentage*	*Examples of Approved Behavior*	*Percentage*
PERSONAL BEHAVIOR PROBLEMS		PERSONAL ACHIEVEMENTS	
Failure to do household chores right	1.4	Helps in household chores	28.3
Scholastic failures	1.4	School work	25.4
Bad personal habits and hygiene (e.g., child is dirty)	3.2	Skills in avocations	4.9
Endanger safety of self	10.6	Personal physical habits and hygiene	2.5
Stay out too late or go too far from home	14.5		
SOCIAL BEHAVIOR PROBLEMS		GOOD SOCIAL BEHAVIOR	
Disobeys parents	17.7	Obeys parents	3.2
Misbehaves with other adults	3.9	Shows good manners or skill in relations with others than parents	4.6
Bad company, tough gang	0.4	Kindness, virtue, etc.	0.7
Destroys property	1.1		
Misbehaves with other children	6.7		
Endangers safety of others	1.1		
Stealing, truancy, etc.	5.3		
Lying, fibbing	1.4		
OTHER ANSWERS		OTHER ANSWERS	
Misbehavior (not further specified)	1.8	Can't think of anything	5.6
Never does wrong things	1.8	Doesn't know what to expect at ten	1.4
		Does good things but what not ascertained	3.9
		Never does anything good	0.4
NOT ASCERTAINED	25.1	NOT ASCERTAINED	19.1

avocational skill as a source of pride and pleasure to most mothers. Cleaning his room or tending a younger sibling or getting good grades in the classroom are more important than the performance of a hobby or the beautifully timed and executed play in a game or on an instrument. These last are not the typical sources of the pleasure of most mothers in their children.

We must precede the findings for another of our questions[25] by repeating our earlier warning that it asks what mothers *should* do; not what they actually do.

Suppose a four-year-old child does something that makes his mother angry and excited. Should the mother punish the child right away while she is angry, or should the mother wait until she is more calm before she decides what to do?

Just over 60 per cent say the mother should wait (though 12.4 per cent of these say they often do not do so themselves). About 37 per cent favor immediate punishment.[26] It seems improbable, and in other studies[27] we find suggestions that it is not the case, that over 60 per cent of Detroit mothers wait until their anger has passed before disciplining their children. The interesting thing here, then, is the prevalence of this procedure as an ideal pattern among our mothers.

The tenor of what most mothers do indicates their conviction that the child must feel and be responsible for his own acts. It will be remembered that we asked what the mother would do if a child of five or six years embarrassed her by his behavior at the table when guests were present.[28] Despite their ideal pattern, about 80 per cent would scold or spank such a child or send him away from the table. Only 16 per cent would try to divert him, explain the problem to him, or ignore the difficulty.[29] The mother is likely, then, to feel that the child must learn to be responsible for his conduct at this early age.

We have some other indications of the timing of demands for responsibility. These appear in the series of questions we asked about the age at which a child should be required to put away his

[25] See Item 21.

[26] In 2.1 per cent of the cases a response was not ascertained. An additional 0.7 per cent of the mothers say they never punish the child and never become angry.

[27] See Daniel R. Miller and Guy E. Swanson, *Inner Conflict and Defense.* To be published by Henry Holt and Co. in 1958.

[28] See Item 32.

[29] In 3.6 per cent of the cases, the mother's response was not ascertained.

own clothes, pick up his own toys, run errands to nearby stores, and dress himself. We chose these activities because all of them might be performed by a young child.[30]

We find that the child between ages two and three has had some demands made for picking up his own toys in most families, that he is typically expected to do something about putting away his clothes and toward dressing himself between ages four and five, and that going to nearby stores will most often be required for the first time at about ages six or seven.

Percentages Required to Perform Certain Tasks at Specified Ages

Age in Years	*Put away Clothes*	*Pick up Toys*	*Run Errands*	*Dress Self*
0, 1	2.8	14.2	*	*
2	12.4	30.7	*	1.1
3	15.5	23.3	4.2	10.6
4	19.8	17.7	8.1	31.1
5	20.5	7.1	20.8	27.6
6	10.6	3.2	23.0	13.1
7 or more	15.3	1.1	42.1	13.1
Never	0.0	0.0	0.4	0.0
Not ascertained	3.2	2.8	1.4	3.5

We also have information on another aspect of teaching the child to be responsible. How long should the mother continue close supervision of the growing child? How long should she continue to keep track of what he is doing most of the time?[31] There are wide differences of opinion.[32] Slightly over 21 per cent of our respondents would stop by the sixth year. Another 18.4 per cent feel that some time between the seventh and the twelfth year is appropriate. The median mother chooses the thirteenth or fourteenth year. A time between fifteen and seventeen years is chosen by 9.8

[30] See Items 13, 13*a*, 13*b*, 13*c*, and 13*d*. [31] See Item 22.

[32] The mother's response was not ascertained for 6.0 per cent of the cases.

per cent. To us, it is surprising that 27.9 per cent say that close supervision should go on for seventeen years or more. This is certainly a large group to feel that the child will not be responsible for himself in late adolescence and young adulthood! It would be important to know if these answers represent the magnitude of the dangers and temptations of urban life as perceived by close to 30 per cent of the population or whether they stand for the inability of these mothers to train children to be capable of handling the experiences presented by their society.

Teaching children to be responsible requires knowledge as well as determination. There are many mothers who wish they knew more about the behavior of children or about methods for making youngsters obey—child dynamics or the control of children. We inquired whether there were any times in the last month when the mother wanted such information.[33] Forty-one and a half per cent answered, "Never." Almost 15 per cent wanted it once or twice. Forty-one per cent would have liked it three or more times.[34] Perhaps the most striking thing about these figures, at least to those accustomed to seeing parents who are highly self-conscious about their handling of children and greatly in doubt about the correctness of their methods, is the large number of mothers who reported no such feelings in the last month. We were less surprised to find that about two-thirds of those who wanted information were interested in learning how to control and direct the child, a third in understanding his expectations and needs. Most parents still find that their problems arise in adapting the child to their standards, not in fitting their behavior to his developing interests and desires.

Finally, we were interested in the number of families in which the parents disagreed about the standards and methods used in "making the child mind."[35] Of those families with a husband in

[33] See Items 24, *24a*, and *24b*.

[34] Another 5.5 per cent said, "Sometimes," while 2.7 per cent said, "Never," but indicated that they regularly read books and articles on child care. The responses of another 2.7 per cent were not ascertained.

[35] See Item 23.

the household, about four mothers reported disagreement to every five who said it did not occur. Although the disagreements cited vary greatly in character, the father was commonly reported as more rigid in the scope and height of the standards he sets and in the severity of the methods he prefers to use for their enforcement. We choose not to make too much of this result, however, since it is highly susceptible to distortion by mothers wanting to make a favorable impression on the interviewer.

SEXUAL EXPLORATION

Children develop attitudes toward sexual behavior considerably before the thirteenth year, or before puberty. We have compared social classes and the integration settings with respect to methods of child care related to sexual exploration. Now we give the findings for the general population of the Detroit area.

We asked parents how they reacted when the young child explored his genitals or tried to follow his mother or father into the bathroom. Specifically, we asked if, at or before age five, he had touched his sex organs and whether the parents did something when this happened.[36] About 58 per cent of the mothers said that their children had not touched their genitals. Some 34 per cent said their children had. The percentage of cases for which the information was not obtained due to interviewer forgetfulness or reticence seems high. It is 7.6 per cent.

Of those parents who said that the child had touched his sex organs, about the same number said they had done something about it as said they did nothing about it. Of the 17 per cent of the population who said it had happened and that they had done something, 5 per cent diverted the child's attention, 7 per cent used gentle physical prevention or talked with the child, 2 per cent administered physical punishment, 2 per cent used shame or ridicule, and 1 per cent threatened or scolded.

[36] See Items 7 and *7a*.

If these figures may be believed, they show a level of tolerance that would not have been anticipated from many of the descriptions of American parents' attitudes toward sexual exploration. We are, of course, rather suspicious of the large number who say they never saw their child explore his genitals. Reports from clinical and hospital studies and from observations in nursery schools and kindergartens suggest that such exploration is almost, if not completely, universal.

Similarly, we are skeptical about the finding that one-third of the mothers with children old enough to have tried to accompany them to the bathroom say their youngsters never did so. Of those who said it had happened, about two out of five prevented the child's entrance and, of those permitting it, about one out of three admitted the youngster only with parents of the same sex.[37]

INDEPENDENCE AND ASSUMING A SEX ROLE

For this early period of childhood, we have already reported the use of a question about the mother's willingness to leave a three-year-old boy with a competent sitter for two afternoons a week. We considered this question as providing a kind of index to her feelings about the desirability of the child's not becoming too dependent on her and about her desire for independence from the child. Some 22.4 per cent of the mothers did not feel that it would be wise to leave a child with a sitter for so long a time.[38] Most of these said that no one but the mother is really suitable to care for a three-year-old child. Only about one out of nine suggested that the child would not like being with strangers. Of the 75.6 per cent of our mothers who felt it would be all right to let such a sitter take care of the youngster, about a third emphasized that it would be good for the mother,

[37] See Items 8 and 8*a*.

[38] See Items 9 and 9*a*. In 2.0 per cent of the cases, the mother's response was not ascertained.

providing her with relaxation, refreshment, new interests and perspectives, freedom for other responsibilities, greater appreciation for the child, or an increase in the child's appreciation for his mother. The considerable majority of the others emphasized the necessity that the child learn to be independent of the mother and to adapt to other people.

Another question involving this theme of independence asked if children should be put on their own as early as possible to work out their own problems.[39] About 43 per cent of these mothers

Specialization of Adult Roles by Sex

PERFORMED BY	*Paint Rooms in House*	*Get Up at Night with Children*	*Decide on Holidays and Celebrations*	*Punish Children*	*Choose Costly Purchases*	*Wash Dishes*
Husband	43.5	3.8	8.9	5.3	12.7	1.9
Wife	12.7	60.3	11.3	29.9	10.3	70.1
Both	39.2	33.7	76.1	61.3	74.4	24.6
Neither	2.4	0.2	0.5	0.9	0.0	1.0
Not ascertained	2.2	2.1	3.1	2.6	2.6	2.4
TOTAL	100.0	100.1	99.9	100.0	100.0	100.0

thought they should. Forty-six and a half per cent disagreed. Over 7 per cent could not make up their minds.[40]

The parents of our children show considerable variation from issue to issue in the extent to which both mother and father undertake an activity or to which it is specialized in the hands of one or the other.[41] There are, then, many different models of appropriate sex-related adult behavior available in this population.

Such activities as punishing the children or choosing where to go and what to do on holidays or deciding about an expensive purchase are usually shared activities. Others, like painting rooms,

[39] See Item 10.

[40] In 3.3 per cent of the cases, a response was not ascertained.

[41] See Items 35, 35*a*, 35*b*, 35*c*, 35*d*, 35*e*, and 35*f*.

getting up at night with children, or washing the dishes are primarily the work of one sex or the other. A large proportion of mothers answer "both" to each of these questions.

We also asked questions about tasks that might be done regularly by adolescent boys and girls.[42]

Specialization of Adolescent Roles by Sex

PERFORMED BY	*Shoveling Walks*	*Washing the Car*	*Dusting Furniture*	*Fixing Light Cords*	*Making Beds*
Boy	64.2	64.2	1.3	52.5	0.7
Girl	0.0	0.3	64.5	0.7	52.2
Both	33.1	28.4	32.1	12.7	45.1
Neither	1.0	5.3	0.7	32.4	0.7
Not ascertained	1.7	1.7	1.3	1.7	1.3
TOTAL	100.0	99.9	99.9	100.0	100.0

In these data, more clearly than in those for adults, it appears that the proportion of parents feeling that tasks may be performed equally by both sexes is about the same whether the behavior was traditionally associated, as in dusting furniture, with the female role, or as in the case of shoveling walks, with the male role in American society. It is still true, however, that, in every case, a majority of mothers try to preserve the differences between the sexes. The boy or girl whose performance of these five activities does not follow traditional patterns can still expect censure in many homes.

MOTHERS' EXPECTATIONS ABOUT THEIR CHILDREN'S ADULT ROLES

Most parents take into account the period when their children will be adults. Fathers and mothers develop expectations about that

[42] See Items 11, 11*a*, 11*b*, 11*c*, 11*d*, and 11*e*.

future period even when their youngsters are small. That future sets the upper bounds of the period of dependency in which the parents have very large and special commitments to the individual child. About 28 per cent of the mothers in the Detroit area think that their children will be able to assume the responsibilities of marriage by the age of twenty.[43] But 21.5 per cent pick twenty-one years, the most popular choice, as the critical point, while 48.7 per cent feel that marriage must be postponed to a later date.[44]

Another device for recording the upper boundary of the parents' expectation of having some large commitments to the child is the age at which he is thought old enough to be a good parent.[45] In answering this question, only 18.4 per cent said twenty years and only 9.5 per cent said twenty-one. The remainder—the majority of parents—were divided equally into the 33.2 per cent favoring ages twenty-two through twenty-four and the same proportion preferring twenty-five years and over.[46] Clearly these ages of marriage are far later than those permitted by the common law in many states and, of course, later than is customary in most nonliterate societies. This practice of late marriage reflects the long-term tendency for the age of dependency and semidependency to be extended upward as training requirements in the occupational fields are enlarged. It is also interesting that a sizable proportion of the population, 33.2 per cent, thinks that the right age for parenthood is two or more years beyond that of marriage.[47] Knowing whether this difference in age of marriage and parenthood represents a period in which the marriage is expected to "settle down" and be ready

[43] See Item 28. It is of interest that the median age at which American men get married was 22.6 years in 1951. The median age, at marriage, of American females was 20.4 years. These figures are taken from: United States Bureau of the Census, *Current Population Reports, Population Characteristics,* Series P-20, No. 38, April 29, 1952, 3.

[44] The mother's response was not ascertained in 1.5 per cent of the cases.

[45] See Item 29.

[46] The mother's response was not ascertained in 5.6 per cent of the cases.

[47] An additional 4.2 per cent placed the age of parenthood *before* the age of marriage while, in 6.7 per cent of the cases, no response was ascertained.

for children, or whether it is a last gay fling before the parents are "tied down" to a family, would help us understand much about the process by which people move from youth to adulthood in our society and the spirit in which they meet the coming of children. The pleasure of most mothers at the coming of new babies seems to favor the first rather than the second of these explanations.

The choice of an occupation is another part of the child's future to which most parents give a lot of thought. We asked for the mothers' best guess in the matter,[48] giving them a choice between what are essentially head and hand occupations. Some 77.3 per cent said their children would have an office job. Almost 5 per cent would not venture a guess.[49] Only 13.1 per cent thought the child would have a factory job. In a population of parents in which 65.3 per cent of the fathers have blue-collar jobs and 68.6 per cent of the grandfathers were similarly employed, this is a startling finding. It holds as true for mothers' guesses about boys as about girls. Clearly, there are hopes here which cannnot possibly be realized, hopes that reflect the prestige and power of the white-collar position in American life. There must be powerful frustrations for blue-collar workers whose parents fostered in them the hope of having a different occupation.

We also asked the mothers in our sample about their feelings concerning the relative importance of a child's being able to use the kind of conceptual skills—skills of thinking and planning and administering—that usually accompany white-collar work as compared with the more motoric or muscular skills of exercising and of working with the hands commonly involved in blue-collar work. This is an item for which we are especially sorry we do not have comparable answers for fathers, since the emphasis on physical skills, particularly for boys, may be quite different for mothers and fathers. However, the mother's feelings are also important and, for the general population, reflect the importance of those talents that lead to the more powerful and prestigeful positions in Ameri-

[48] See Item 27.

[49] In 4.8 per cent of the cases, the mother's response was not ascertained.

can life. About 80 per cent of our respondents preferred to have their children involved in activities which teach them to think, plan, or organize, while 16.7 per cent favored activities which develop the child's physique or give him plenty of exercise.[50]

We also have some information about the skills which mothers feel are needed in the world of work.[51] With reference to office or clerical work and to work in factories, we asked, "if a person wants to make money on a job . . . , is it more important for him to have the right kind of personality, or to know how to do that kind of work well?" Only 11.1 per cent said personality was most important for monetary success in the factory, while 38.5 per cent chose it for the office situations.[52] But in two-thirds of the cases saying "personality" for either setting, the reason given is that a man's personality affects his chance of getting and keeping a job. Our respondents did not see "the right kind of personality" as desirable because it brings one the personal gratifications of popularity. It is the employable personality, not the personality that brings interpersonal satisfactions, which is usually seen as required on the job.

And what of these parents' views of life's gratifications? It should not be thought, as some novelists of this century like to believe, that modern parents are robots, shaped only for the desk or lathe, and little better than their pencils or machines. Their personal interests are not stifled. They do not advocate that children stifle theirs.

We asked each mother in our sample whether she would encourage her child to follow his own interests or those of others, assuming that both were equally worthwhile.[53] We also asked her to assume that, if he followed his own desires, he would have little

50 See Items 12, 12*a,* and 12*b*. Responses for 4.0 per cent of the cases were not ascertained.

51 See Items 25, 25*a,* 25*b,* 26, 26*a,* and 26*b.*

52 In the office situation, 4.7 per cent gave indecisive answers as did 3.3 per cent in the factory situation. The respective percentages of cases for which a response was not ascertained are 0.9 and 1.2.

53 See Item 31.

time to spend with other children. Just over 60 per cent of the mothers said they would encourage the child to do what he liked. Only 36.5 per cent said that they would try to get him to go along with others' wishes.[54] Most of the mothers in this minority made their choice on the grounds that the child does not know his long-term advantage, that he will want friends and the joy and help they provide, and that he will take pleasure in being able to handle people with ease.

Further, most of these mothers are able to enjoy life's pleasures as they come. Present gratification need not always be postponed in order to prepare for the future. We find that 56.9 per cent of the mothers chose their preferred leisure activities for the inherent gratification those activities offer. Another 10.6 per cent said that the gratifications they got from leisure were both immediate and longer-term benefits. Only 10.3 per cent chose their leisure preferences because they were sound investments for future gains.[55]

Finally, a mother's children play a vital part in her future happiness. Unless our mothers were grossly unable to report their real feelings, there is clear evidence that the greater part of them would feel real regret if, after the child was grown, they were unable to see him.[56] Seventy-two per cent would be very lonely and upset. About 15 per cent would be unhappy, but feel they would adjust to the situation. Five per cent said the separation would not make much difference.[57] The emotional investment of mothers in their children is obvious when pointed out, but it is sometimes forgotten in an emphasis on the dependence of the child on the parent.

[54] Responses for 2.4 per cent of the cases were not ascertained.

[55] See Items 33 and 33*a*. Another 8.4 per cent said they wanted to do the things they chose for leisure pursuits because they did not get to do them now; 3.1 per cent gave miscellaneous reasons. Responses were not ascertained for 10.6 per cent of the cases.

[56] See Item 34.

[57] Responses were not ascertained for 3.3 per cent of the cases.

CONCLUSION

This composite picture of Detroit's families is not easily summarized. With rare exceptions, it reveals a considerable range of methods for rearing youngsters and of attitudes toward them. Of course, that very range of practices provokes the growth of knowledge, for it stands as a reminder that the social world is always richer in its complexity than our schemes and explanations suggest. We have offered these findings with the hope that they will stimulate work which will enlarge the scope of our understanding.

SELECTED BIBLIOGRAPHY

BELL, ROBERT R., and BUERKLE, JACK V., "Mother-Daughter Conflict During the 'Launching Stage.'" *Marriage and Family Living* (November, 1962), pp. 384–88.

BURCHINAL, LEE G., and ROSSMAN, JACK E., "Relations Among Maternal Employment Indices and Developmental Characteristics of Children." *Marriage and Family Living* (November, 1961), pp. 334–39.

DAGER, EDWARD Z., "Socialization and Personality Development in the Child," in Harold T. Christensen, ed., *Handbook of Marriage and the Family* (Chicago: Rand McNally & Co., 1964), pp. 740–81.

DAVIS, KINGSLEY, "The Sociology of Parent-Child Conflict." *American Sociological Review* (August, 1950), pp. 523–35.

GLICK, PAUL, "The Family Cycle." *American Sociological Review* (April, 1947), pp. 164–74.

KAGAN, JEROME, "The Child's Perception of the Parent," in Jerome M. Seidman, ed., *The Child* (New York: Holt, Rinehart & Winston, Inc., 1958), pp. 138–40.

KELL, LEONE, and ALDOUS, JOAN, "Trends in Child Care Over Three Generations." *Marriage and Family Living* (May, 1960), pp. 176–77.

FAMILY AND CLASS DYNAMICS IN MENTAL ILLNESS

Jerome K. Myers and Bertram H. Roberts

Childbearing and childrearing have presented parents in societies past and present with a variety of personal and social obligations. By definition, the first function of parents is simply that of reproduction. It has generally been accepted by societies that reproduction should be a function of marriage, and taboos of varying strengths against birth outside of marriage have been developed to keep the reproductive function within marriage. In addition, societies have almost always delegated to the parents—especially the mother—the responsibility for meeting the needs of the infant. The parents continue to have the child dependent on them until he reaches the social age of independence. A third—and very important—obligation of the parents is that they make the child a functioning member of society. When a child proves unable to

---

function within the minimal expectations of society, the parents are generally held responsible for the child's inadequacy.

But, while the parents must accept much of the responsibility as agents of society, they cannot be held completely responsible; it is also necessary to consider various agencies of society and, further, society itself. Through society—through both the agencies and agents it has built in—the newborn infant undergoes socialization. This process of socialization is not only important for the development of each individual, but it is also necessary to a society's future. For a society to continue, it must have institutionalized means for training the young to take on positive social attitudes.

It is true that the basic functions of childrearing can be met by other agencies of society, and occasionally there have been societies that have done this; but usually the childrearing function has been filled by the parents. Because the parent-child relationship has been in existence so long in all societies, many view it as "natural" rather than socially determined. Historically it has been assumed that, if adults were capable of having children, they were capable of rearing them. The fact that many adults in all societies are poor parents, by any criteria, is generally ignored. In most cultures of the world, including the United States, society will intervene in the parent-child relationship only under the most extreme circumstances. In most respects, the "rights" of parents over their children are far more extensive than any other "rights" that one group of individuals have over another group.

Becoming parents for the first time is probably the most significant and demanding role that most individuals encounter during their lifetime and the new experience calls for an extended emotional involvement. This event has different demands on the role of the mother and the role of the father, though it should be emphasized that they each derive an important part of their meaning in relationship to the other. While the parent-child relationship is important, there is another influential relationship in childrearing—the mother-father relationship. This is important not only as a division of labor and responsibility, but also for buttressing their relationship with the children as a pair of "parents." For example, a mother and father who do not support each other in their roles as parents may create confusion for the children or set up a situation where the children play one parent off against the other.

In the selection that follows the authors examine the family as the possible "root" or cause of the mental health problems of the offspring. The method used by the two researchers was a "controlled case study" approach, and they state that their method combines the features of the breadth found in the statistical survey and the depth of the case study analysis. The study they evolved from this combination is one based on a relatively small number of cases that could be interviewed in depth according to a standardized schedule. The data reported here are based on the responses of fifty patients in the age range of 22–44. The major sociological variable of the analysis was social class; and the two social class levels that were used were lower middle class (Class III) and lower lower class (Class V). The major psychological variable of their analysis was the diagnosis of the patient's mental health as either schizophrenic or psychoneurotic. The following table has divided cases according to the variables of sex, social class, and mental illness diagnosis:

	CLASS III		CLASS V	
	Males	*Females*	*Males*	*Females*
Schizophrenics	7	6	6	6
Psychoneurotics	6	7	6	6
Totals	13	13	12	12

It seems clear that the one limitation of this study is the small number of cases investigated. But the study is valuable, because it provides both some empirically supported insights into parent-child relationships and the possible connection of this relationship to the occurrence of mental health problems.

This research was undertaken to examine the two general hypotheses that (1) social and psychodynamic factors in the development of psychiatric disorders are correlative to an individual's position in the class structure; and (2) mobility in the class structure is associated with the development of psychiatric disorders. We selected for study white, adult patients from two nonadjacent social classes, III and V, and from two diagnostic groups, schizophrenia and psychoneurosis. We examined the hypotheses in several ways. We determined if there were (1) class differences in social, psychodynamic, and mobility factors in the patients' development; (2) differences in the experiences of schizophrenic and neurotic patients at each class level; and (3) differences in the social and dynamic experiences of schizophrenics and neurotics which cut across class lines.

Our findings supported the first hypothesis. We discovered significant differences between the experiences of class III and class V patients in the following areas: intrafamilial role relationships, sex role development, external community presses, attitudes toward psychiatric illness, the therapy process, and symptomatology. More important for an examination of the hypothesis, presses and stresses at each class level were found more frequently and with greater intensity among the schizophrenic than among the neurotic patients. Our second hypothesis was partially supported, since mobility was associated with the development of psychiatric disorders in class III but not in class V, and it occurred to a greater extent among class III schizophrenics than neurotics. However, the very fact that mobility was not related to psychiatric illnesses in class V further supported our first hypothesis. It demonstrated that this important social factor in psychiatric illnesses was associated with the position of patients in the class structure.

In interpreting our findings or applying them to another community, several limitations should be recognized. *First,* our sample was a small and selected population from one community. It was limited to two social classes, two functional disorders, white adult patients between the ages of 22 and 44, and to patients, families, and therapists willing to cooperate. We do not know, for example, if our hypotheses would have been supported had other classes or diagnostic groups been studied. *Second,* we studied *treated* mental disorders, and we cannot determine if our results would have applied to persons who were not receiving psychiatric treatment, but were in need of it. *Third,* we did not have a control group of "normal" persons, so we could not test our hypotheses definitively. *Fourth,* our data were based upon recall and were subject to the shortcomings of this method. However, we attempted to increase the validity and reliability of the data by utilizing several informants in each case. *Fifth,* we had little data on infancy and early childhood until age six or seven. Much of our material for this period was based upon general statements about childhood experiences. *Finally,* the social and psychiatric characteristics associated with a given social class or diagnostic group did not necessarily apply to every patient in that group. We described characteristics which occurred more frequently in one class or diagnostic group than in another, but we do not imply that these tendencies were found among all persons in such a group; nor do we imply that these tendencies were entirely absent among all members of the comparison group. We described characteristics found among more than half of the patients in one group and among significantly more patients than among the comparison group. Thus, some of the characteristics found among the majority of patients in one group, class III for example, were usually found among a minority of the patients in the comparison group, class V in this case.

ETIOLOGICAL CONSIDERATIONS

The reader should not interpret our emphasis upon social class as meaning we consider it the only or the most important factor related to the development of psychiatric illnesses. Although little is known about the etiology of functional mental illness, multiple and interrelated factors seem involved. Research and clinical evidence suggest that some of these factors are constitutional, organic, intrapsychic, and interpersonal in nature as well as environmental. For example, there may be certain constitutional predispositions to functional psychiatric illness. Such factors may have been responsible for the shy and withdrawn personalities of the schizophrenic patients we studied. On the other hand, the way such persons are treated by others may be a factor in determining if and when inherent tendencies develop. Perhaps, less external pressure is necessary for the development of psychiatric disorders among persons endowed with certain constitutional weaknesses. Or, organic predispositions may develop differentially into clinical illness under varying social and interpersonal conditions.

Since we studied only one part of the social environment and did not have a control group of "normal" persons, we cannot hope to make any definitive statements about etiology. Certainly, social class variables alone do not explain the cause of psychiatric illness, for it is found at all social levels. However, so little is known about the cause of functional mental disorder that we believe research is needed on many fronts. We chose to study in detail the influence of social class factors.

Our findings demonstrate that life conditions differed in classes III and V. Certain of these differentiating intrafamilial and community conditions were found among more schizophrenic than neurotic patients at each class level. Because of their association with a more serious functional illness, schizophrenia, we termed these conditions, "presses." Thus, there were class differences in the presses and resultant stresses which differentiated schizophrenic and neurotic patients, suggesting that the paths to psychiatric illnesses may differ in classes III and V. Also, certain presses conducive to a more serious functional illness, schizophrenia, may be more common in class V than in class III. For example, many of the life conditions associated with the development of schizophrenia in both classes were more common in the histories of class V than class III neurotics.

Social class did not seem to be a *direct cause* of psychiatric illness. Rather, living at a given social level apparently helped to determine the probability of a patient's exposure to certain presses and development of certain stresses. It affected the patients' familial and community experiences, such as types of interpersonal relationships, family roles, opportunities for employment, and mobility experiences. Living under such differing life conditions also may have affected differentially the patients' intrapsychic processes and ego development which seem more directly related to the development of functional mental illness.

Our class approach was molar. It told us little about why certain persons at a given level became ill but not others, or why the patients and not their siblings developed psychiatric disorders. We consider our approach a valid first step, however, because of the paucity of knowledge about the etiology of functional mental illness. Granting that there are many etiological factors, our findings demonstrate that social class variables were related to the development of mental illness among the patients we studied. We turn next to a discussion of this relationship.

SUMMARY AND INTERPRETATION OF FINDINGS

[W]e have presented data on various aspects of family dynamics and community factors associated with the development of mental illness. Certain trends which run through these materials will now be presented. At each class level certain presses and stresses were found among more schizophrenic than neurotic patients, indicating that they were not only class-related but associated with the development of the more serious psychiatric illness.

Class III Patients

Two values highly held in class III, respectability and success, figured prominently in the patients' socialization. They permeated all aspects of class III culture, influencing intrafamilial as well as community relationships. They represented lifelong presses for significantly more class III than class V patients. From birth, most class III patients were taught to focus all their efforts and energies upon social acceptance and upward mobility.

The first impact of these presses upon class III patients was through family role relationships and child-rearing practices. Most parents projected their frustrated mobility aspirations upon the patients and prepared the patients to accomplish what they themselves were unable to. Maternal supervision was rigid and demanding. The patients had to learn to curb their instinctual aggressive and sexual impulses. They were required to respect and conform to the demands of their elders. Their parents generally controlled their behavior closely. By the time most patients entered school they were well-motivated to behave in a socially acceptable fashion and be successful in order to please their elders.

Their parents' values were reinforced by persons the patients contacted outside their families. Teachers, ministers, Sunday School teachers, and others set high moral standards for them. They were continually taught to supplant crudeness, violence, aggression, and the expression of sexual desires with "socially approved," that is, inhibited, behavior. The above adults also supported the patients' mobility aspirations. By late childhood most patients had accepted and internalized well the basic values of their class culture.

During adolescence, these presses upon the patients led to a movement away from their parents, as the patients set high standards for themselves. Few parents could afford the education the patients desired, so most patients had to compromise their educational aims. Although they achieved more than their brothers and sisters, few patients were able to attain their educational goals. In adulthood, they were successful by class III standards, but the mobility values they held had led the patients to social and economic aspirations which were beyond class III standards and which they could not attain.

These class III presses gave rise to three particular types of stress. *First,* class III patients experienced between their instinct-drives and moral values more conflicts than most class V patients. The majority of class III patients internalized the value of respectability so well that it became part of their conscience and its unconscious counterpart, the superego. Throughout their lives they denied themselves the immediate gratification of many sensual desires which they consciously or unconsciously believed would handicap their mobility efforts in hopes of attaining future rewards. They were more likely to check their aggressive and sex impulses or express them by way of compromise than class V patients who expressed them more directly and with less restraint.

Our data suggest that class III patients had stricter superegos than class V patients, and that they internalized social inhibitions more strongly. Parental discipline in class III was firm, consistent, and more effective. The parents' own inhibited behavior and strict superegos seemed to serve as models for the patients, documenting Freud's view that the superego of the child is built upon the model of the parents' superegos as well as upon their behavior. The very fact that class III patients were less rebellious and more conforming in their behavior may indicate their early internalization of social norms and development of effective superegos.

The conflict between moral values and instinct drives began in infancy when the class III patients' mothers implemented class values in their rearing procedures. During this period the aggression of class III patients was probably thwarted more frequently than that of class V patients. According to psychoanalytic theory, a fixation during the second year of life is related to the later development of such compulsive character traits as orderliness, rigidity, cleanliness, punctuality, and perfection. We could not test this proposition, but it was interesting that such traits as well as obsessive-compulsive psychiatric symptoms were more common among class III than among class V patients. This class differential may well be related to the fact that class III mothers more frequently emphasized such traits in their rearing procedures. Probably early in life the patients began to internalize these values; even in infancy they may have begun experiencing more conflict than most class V patients between their internal drives and these social values. Certainly, they became more inhibited than class V patients in childhood in their attempts to behave "properly." Frequently, class III patients could not enjoy themselves as lower status patients did for fear of engaging in "unacceptable" behavior themselves. They apparently suffered more often from frustration of their instinctual impulses accompanied by some anxiety.

Probably the greatest conflict between moral values and impulsive behavior occurred in the sexual area. This began with the pregenital drives of infancy. In early childhood from the third through the sixth year of life, infantile sex drives become more intense. At this phase of the life cycle, as Freud pointed out, there appears to be a flowering of infant sexuality with the parent of the opposite sex as the main love object and the parent of the same sex as the chief rival. According to psychoanalytic theory, the child experiences anxiety and later guilt in such relationships, derived from a fear of injury to the genitalia. Unfortunately, we had little data in our study on this phase of the life cycle. Most of these processes are unconscious and may reveal themselves only by symptoms and inhibitions which represent symbolic substitutes of unresolved conflicts in this area. However, these phenomena appeared to be intensified in the small, more tightly knit class III family. . . . [T]he classic parent-child relationships in sex role development were more intense in class III than in class V. Families were so large and home conditions so disorganized in the lower class that generally such relationships had less chance to develop to the same degree.

During later childhood, from about the sixth year until puberty, the patients' sex drives were dormant, so there was minimal conflict between them and their moral values. However, in adolescence there was a strong resurgence of the sexual drive which had a definite genital character, and, despite their training and values, many class III patients engaged in sexual activities contrary to the moral standards of their class. Many patients apparently satisfied their biological drives through premarital sexual intercourse at the expense of violating their moral sexual codes. They became ashamed of their behavior and were fearful that their parents would learn about it. Their shame led to deep guilt feelings, for they could not change their moral values as easily as their behavior. Although patients in both classes experienced some difficulty, class III patients experienced more anxiety about their adolescent and premarital sex behavior. . . .

Second, the inability of class III patients to live up to the values they had internalized was very stressful. The achievement of respectability and success was such an important value that the patients became extremely frustrated if they could not attain these goals. When their behavior did not measure up to these standards they were likely to develop serious inner conflicts, manifested as feelings of shame and guilt. This pattern could be traced during the typical patient's entire lifetime.

During childhood, most class III patients experienced mild anxieties when they could not satisfy their mothers' demands. Most patients at this level also had difficulty respecting their fathers because of their mothers' dominant position in the home. Problems of respect for both parents increased in adolescence. The patients became ashamed of their parents and felt handicapped by their parents' status in their mobility efforts. Since the patients had so well internalized their class value that children owe respect and obedience to their parents, they felt extremely guilty about their behavior.

Related to this problem were the patients' efforts to become independent of their mothers' control. During childhood their mothers' control was such that the patients became dependent upon them. However, to be successfully mobile in adolescence and adulthood, they had to break away from their mothers' control and establish their independence. Not only was the typical class III patient's dependency needs deeply ingrained by then, but any movement away from his mother represented a failure to comply with her wishes that he remain dependent. Thus, most patients faced a serious dilemma. To be successful they had to establish their independence from their mothers, but they were likely to develop guilt feelings for not complying with their wishes.

Even more stressful was the patients' failure to attain their mobility goals. When they realized that their past sacrifices had not been sufficient to ensure their lifelong aim of successful mobility, most patients became extremely frustrated and anxious, followed by severe guilt feelings over their failure.

Third, class III patients were under constant tension because of their mobility efforts. As they moved upward in the social structure, they had to modify continually their behavior to conform to the standards of their new status group. They could not relax or fall back upon the behavior they had learned in childhood, because it might have been inappropriate and detrimental to their efforts. They always had to be conscious of their role performance; the tension never let up. Furthermore, in their upward mobility most patients alienated their families and former friends, but they were never fully accepted by the groups to which they aspired. They occupied almost permanent "marginal" positions in society.

Accepting values such as respectability and responsibility, class III patients were less likely than class V patients to express their frustration in aggressive, hostile, or violent behavior. Instead, they were more likely to turn it inward into psychological conflict. They appeared more sensitive to internal threats, fears, guilts, and conflicts than the lower-class patients. When stresses became so great that they were expressed in psychiatric symptoms, class III patients more frequently selected psychological, subjective, and personal symptoms to express their inner conflict. They displayed more intense feelings of shame, guilt, and inner conflict than class V patients.

Sex differences were superimposed upon the basic class III patterns of press and stress. Most class III patients assumed roles which differed somewhat from those expected of their sex. Female patients, accepting fully the values of mobility and sexual equality of opportunity, aspired to professional or business careers which were difficult for girls to attain at their social level. Their desire for success was so great that most undertook higher education, although they received little financial aid because of the limited resources of their parents.

Identifying closely with their fathers, most class III female patients incorporated certain masculine values and behavior characteristics into their roles. They were active and aggressive, striving to establish their independence from their families. Most experienced deep conflicts between a career and marriage, and they resisted the traditional role of marriage to a man of their own background. Each female patient achieved as much or more than her brothers and sisters educationally and occupationally, but was dissatisfied with her achievements which fell far short of her goals.

The typical male patient in class III never developed the masculine and aggressive characteristics necessary for occupational success. He identified with many of his mother's feminine values and developed intellectual and passive interests. He was successful academically, but his dependency upon his mother hindered his development of the initiative and independence necessary for masculine success.

We could not determine if the behavior of patients was due to innate tendencies, interpersonal relations, social conditions, or a combination of these factors. Regardless of the cause, patients of both sexes assumed roles which conflicted with those expected of them. The ensuing conflicts and frustrations intensified the stresses they were already under as mobile persons.

Class V Patients

External presses in class V differed markedly from those found in class III. Two presses, adverse economic conditions and isolation from community institutions, permeated all aspects of class V culture. Parents made little or no effort to have the patients focus their efforts upon attaining the higher status goals of respectability and success. Economic pressures were so extreme that most of the parents' energies went into satisfying the needs of daily living. They had little time or energy to train the patients according to middle-class standards.

Within the family parental control of children was minimal, and class V patients received little warmth or affection. Little effort was made to have the patients curb their impulsive behavior. They were reared in an environment where violence, aggression, hostility, and rebellion were accepted. Most patients observed their parents' isolation from community institutions and their hostility toward authority. Before the patients even entered school, they had acquired their parents' philosophy that one must look out for one's own interests or else be exploited.

In school most class V patients impressed their teachers unfavorably, and in turn they were treated badly as their parents had predicted. They were rebuffed in the few attempts they made to be accepted socially, so most remained isolated from social and religious institutions for the rest of their lives.

Their parents' failure was transferred to the patients. Because of the extremely adverse economic conditions under which they were reared, they had little chance of success. Not only did the patients' lack of focus upon respectability hamper any mobility aspirations they might possess, but the very values they learned were a decided handicap. Society instilled in them the desire for luxuries which higher status children took for granted, but it provided little opportunity for the patients to obtain them. They had to work at an early age if they were to acquire the money to satisfy any of their culturally acquired drives. However, their desire to earn money and their understandable inability to see the relevance of education for future occupational opportunities led to the patients' leaving school as soon as possible. Their job horizons and opportunities, therefore, were so severely limited that they could never escape economic pressures.

These presses gave rise to distinctive patterns of stress in class V. *First,* most class V patients were reared in an environment where there was little love, affection, protection, and stability. Many psychiatrists believe that lack of loving care and affection in infancy may result in unfortunate consequences for the child's personality development. Some even believe that major environmental disturbances at this period may result frequently in schizophrenia.

Perhaps the lifelong dependency and characterological states of dejection, apathy and suspicion so common among lower-class patients might have been related to damage at this early phase of the life cycle.

Second, most class V patients were constantly on the defensive in their relationships with their parents. Although generally neglecting the patients, parents made erratic and violent attempts to maintain discipline. This led to fear of their parents, especially their fathers, and to uncertainty of how to behave toward them. The constant fear and uncertainty seemed extremely stressful for many patients and led to problems of ego integration.

Third, class V patients felt neglected and rejected all their lives, first by their parents, brothers, and sisters, and later by the institutional representatives of society and higher status persons in general. They were isolated from close and warm personal contacts. They felt unwanted and uncertain of their goals in life. They lacked the sense of "basic trust" which Erikson believes the child must acquire in infancy from his parents for his healthy personality development. They sought parental substitutes, especially father figures, but they were unsuccessful. Their continual frustration in satisfying their emotional needs and exploitation seemed to lead to a distrust of others. They were suspicious and lacked confidence in human relations. Most class V patients reacted by increasing their hostility and aggression toward others so that their interpersonal relationships deteriorated even further.

Fourth, significantly more class V than class III patients experienced lifelong economic insecurity. In childhood they could rarely satisfy the socially instilled desires for luxuries that other children considered normal needs. They had to struggle all their lives to meet their daily living requirements. Most considered their parents as failures and later regarded themselves in the same manner. They were resentful of their lot and felt trapped by conditions, but were helpless to do anything about it. Despite their feelings they did not blame themselves for their failures nor feel ashamed of them. They simply did not hold the value that one must succeed to be respectable, but instead they blamed society. They felt exploited and "beaten down" by life. In one sense, they reacted by resignation to their fate, but their aggressive, hostile, suspicious, and antisocial behavior represented another reaction. The constant press of adverse economic conditions seemed to produce in the patients vague and generalized feelings of insecurity. If class V parents had provided warm and affectionate home environments and had not neglected the patients, these feelings might not have been as severe. However, the parents' inability to provide either economic or emotional security for the patients led to a sense of "not belonging" or of being "lost."

Finally, the class V patients' more direct expression of their instinctual impulses resulted in certain stresses. Class V patients seemed to have less strict egos than class III patients. They seemed less able to check their own impulses and to master the harsh reality aspects of their lives. It is true that compared to class III patients, their more immediate gratification of their impulses led to less inhibition, fewer immediate frustrations, and less conflict with their moral values. However, in a society where there is a considerable emphasis upon deferred gratifications of instinctual desires, this led to other problems. Middle- and upper-class persons who control our societal institutions did not accept the class V pattern of immediate impulse gratification. Consequently, lower-class patients were in constant conflict with the institutional representatives of society such as teachers, police, social workers, clergymen, and employers. These persons viewed such class V impulse gratification negatively, labeling it as "bad," "immoral," "irresponsible," "antisocial," etc. The class V pattern also led to an immature sense of societal obligation and to a selfish view of life. Because of his paramount concern for his own welfare and his suspicion of others, the typical class V patient experienced few satisfying interpersonal relationships.

In sum, external presses bore heavily upon class V patients. Life was harsh and raw for them. They had little cushioning against the rough spots of their environment. Threats to their economic, social, and physical security seemed stronger than in class III. They felt neglected, rejected, exploited, and trapped by unfortunate circumstances. Their reactions to these stresses more frequently took the form of violent and aggressive antisocial behavior, hostility, or psychosomatic symptoms than the feelings of guilt and shame which were so common among class III patients.

Within class V, economic pressures were greater upon male patients and social isolation upon female patients. Male patients had to assume heavy financial responsibilities in early adolescence. Initially, most appeared successful to their families of orientation, but few were able to improve their positions because of their limited training, experience, and opportunities. When viewed by their families as adult roles, their jobs were not valued as highly. In most cases, their families' praise turned to criticism. After marriage, most class V male patients had many children rapidly and so faced lifelong financial pressures.

Although class V female patients did not have to secure jobs at as early an age as males, they had to help with the housework and to care for their younger brothers and sisters. These tasks were more confining than the boys' jobs, and the female patients had relatively little free time. In adolescence most obtained jobs, but they had to continue to help at home. They had few contacts outside the home. After a brief courtship, they were again tied to the house, for most had children soon after marriage. Throughout their lives class V female patients had only limited social contacts beyond their families. Whereas feelings of economic insecurity seemed to overwhelm class V male patients, female patients expressed greater feelings of isolation and neglect.

Diagnostic Differences

The relationship between external press and internal stress in classes III and V seems clear. When the patients were frustrated by the presses of their external environment, they developed internal stresses which were frequently manifested in interpersonal difficulties, antisocial behavior, and psychiatric symptoms. Both intrafamilial and community presses in classes III and V bore more heavily upon schizophrenic than upon neurotic patients. The presses were not only more intense in the schizophrenic patients' development, but they were found among a greater number of such patients. This indicates that the presses we have isolated were indeed stressful as well as class related, for their intensity and frequency were *directly* related to the severity of the psychiatric disorder. It seemed clear that the greater the frustration, the greater the severity of the mental illness.

Our analysis of diagnostic differences in intrafamilial and sex role development presses and stresses, regardless of the patients' class status, sheds further light on the relationship between social class and the development of mental illness. The reader will recall that schizophrenic patients manifested more pathological, psychosocial developmental syndromes than neurotic patients. Briefly, schizophrenics in both classes displayed patterns of submissive and withdrawn behavior. They complied with parental and community authority and were inhibited socially and sexually. At the same time, certain presses bore more heavily upon the schizophrenics than upon the neurotics in both classes. Specifically, most schizophrenic patients had few positive or rewarding contacts with family members. The home was disorganized and full of tension and antagonism. Their parents had psychopathological tendencies which disrupted family affairs. Their mothers showed little genuine interest or affection for the schizophrenic patients. Their fathers were inadequate both at home and in the community, so that their mothers had to assume responsibility for family affairs.

Whatever the factors responsible for the schizophrenics' shy personalities, be they constitutional, social, interpersonal, or other, it was clear that the above presses supported the further development of their deviant adjustments. Feeling neglected and overwhelmed by the chaos of the home, it was easy for the schizophrenics to avoid unpleasantness and seek the affection and guidance they lacked in autistic withdrawal. It was also clear that these presses gave rise to certain common stresses among schizophrenics.

They felt isolated from warm intrafamilial relationships and neglected and rejected by their parents.

It was interesting that many of the intrafamilial presses associated with the development of schizophrenia were associated with class V neurotics but not class III neurotics. Stated another way, class III schizophrenics tended to display more presses characteristic of class V patients in general than did class III neurotics. Specifically, these were the general disorganization of the home, lack of parental affection, guidance, and control, isolation of fathers from the family, heavy responsibility of mothers, and the responsibilities of siblings in the child-rearing process. Similarly, schizophrenics and class V patients, in general, experienced similar stresses—feelings of neglect, rejection, isolation, and fear of parents.

Perhaps, association of certain presses and stresses related to the development of schizophrenia with both schizophrenic and neurotic patients in class V holds a clue to the greater amount of schizophrenia among lower-class groups found in many studies. Perhaps, certain conditions of class V life were conducive to the development of schizophrenia. This does not mean that such conditions were *the cause* of schizophrenia, for persons from all social levels developed this disorder, and not all lower-class persons became schizophrenics. However, it may mean that there existed in class V more conditions conducive to the isolation and withdrawal of the frustrated patient. Many of the community presses at this level, such as isolation from community affairs, as well as the above intrafamilial presses led patients to feelings of isolation, loneliness, neglect, and rejection. Certain external conditions at all levels can lead to to these stresses that are characteristics of schizophrenics, but that these very stresses were common among nearly all class V patients in our study, although to varying degrees, seemed significant. Furthermore, the harshness, hostility, violence, and aggression of the class V environment appeared especially difficult for the somewhat shy and withdrawn persons who later developed schizophrenia. They apparently received less sympathy than the same type of individuals in class III, and they had good reason to withdraw from such an unpleasant environment and seek satisfactions in their fantasies.

IDENTIFICATION

Our data suggest that the differential life conditions and presses under which patients in classes III and V lived may have affected their ego development. Although this process has many facets, we want to discuss that aspect which has been central to our research, namely, identification. Identification, as the reader will recall, refers to the individual's desire to establish or maintain a satisfying self-defining relationship to another person and to the process whereby one person puts himself in the place of another or takes over the role of another. We are interested particularly in the social aspects of the process whereby the individual incorporates into his own role, the values, ideals, and/or behavior of key identification figures in his environment.

Class III Patients

As we have shown, there was more warmth and affection during childhood in the homes of class III than class V patients. Class III patients generally had closer ties with their parents than did lower-class patients, which seemed to be the preparation for a more solid basis for later identification. Although class III patients had some difficulty respecting their fathers because of their mothers' domination, both parents appeared successful when measured in terms of the "generalized others" the patients came in contact with outside of their families. Their mothers were interested in their development and appeared respectable and socially acceptable. Significantly fewer mothers in this class than in class V neglected their families or had to work outside the home. Most class III fathers had steady jobs and provided comfortably for their families. Both parents were active and respectable members of the community. In childhood, then, class III parents provided adequate social models for the patients' behavior and values.

Class III parents provided the patients with mobility aspirations during childhood, without realizing that the acceptance of these values would later lead the patients away from them. Their parents' aspirations were general in nature, lacking in specific details, but in school the patients acquired more definite goals. Generally, such aspirations were far above their parents' social status and ambitions, and during early adolescence most patients became ashamed of their parents, feeling handicapped by their social background. They seemed no longer able to accept either their parents' behavior or their specific values. Since their parents no longer served as models for their ego ideals, that is, the selves the patients wanted to become, they turned to outsiders. At this time the patients' early attachments, dependencies, and identifications with their parents were subjected to a testing.

Many class III patients found role models for their behavior, values, and ego ideals in adults outside their families, such as teachers and parents of higher status schoolmates, but such persons did not seem to satisfy the patients' emotional needs. At this time, class III patients apparently experienced conflicts between values they had learned from their parents and those they had acquired from their higher status peers, teachers, and other adults. The patients' childhood identifications no longer sufficed during this crucial period of "identity formation" in adolescence, to use Erikson's term, and the patients experienced a basic discontinuity in their identifications. Their parents no longer served as suitable identification figures, but few patients could find adequate substitutes.

Class V Patients

Most class V patients received less love and attention from their parents than did class III patients. Their mothers were overburdened with household responsibilities and their fathers were absent but brutal figures. Both parents were so overwhelmed by economic problems that they displayed little interest in the patients. Moreover, there was little stability in the patients' homes. Neglected by their mothers and fearful of their fathers, few patients were able to establish satisfactory relationships with them as a basis for later identifications.

Most patients learned in childhood that other persons held their parents in low esteem, so it was not strange that the patients came to regard their parents as failures. Unable to offer the patients material comforts that other children took for granted the parents could hardly be expected to serve as adequate models for the patients' behavior. Most class V parents could not provide the patients with a consistent set of goals which seemed rewarding; nor could they offer the patients a set of values to which to aspire. In brief, few class V parents provided adequate identification figures for the patients' behavior or ego ideals.

The patients could find few persons in the lower-class environment they wanted to copy as models. Most of the persons they knew well were failures like their parents, held in low esteem by the rest of society. Adults who were institutional representatives of society, like teachers and social workers, rejected the patients. These adults and higher status children also treated the patients as social inferiors. Under these conditions many patients conceived of themselves as inferior, and could not adequately develop or maintain their self-respect.

Unable to idealize persons they knew because they were failures, the patients sought as models distant and glamorous figures outside their environment, such as movie stars and athletes. Some class III patients also identified with such persons at times, but they did not retain this pattern. However, most class V patients did, but since these persons did not provide realistic role models for their behavior, the patients could hardly copy them successfully. The patients' constant but unsuccessful search for parental surrogates seemed indicative of their lack of suitable childhood identification figures.

In some cases, particularly among males, peer group members seemed to provide more available role models for the patients than their parents. The patients' identification with peers and the lack of satisfactory adult figures might have been related to their lack of responsibility later in life. It was difficult for patients to assume a responsible adult role when there were so few persons in their immediate environment to act as models. The class V patients' problems in ego formation at the end of adolescence seemed to grow out of their lack of suitable childhood identifications rather than out of discontinuity in identifications as was the case in class III. Most class V patients were never able to identify with "socially acceptable" models, that is, models approved by higher status persons.

Compared to class III patients, most class V patients seemed to have defective superegos. Although they were exposed more than class III patients to external methods of discipline, such as physical and often brutal punishment, they did not seem to internalize social inhibitions to as great a degree. Several conditions considered important for the development of an effective conscience and superego seemed to be missing in class V families. Parents showed little love for the patients, so that they felt unwanted and rejected; neither did the parents define right and wrong for the patients' personality development. Punishments and rewards were erratic, based upon the parents' mood and temper. Neither parents nor other adults ever presented any role models of firm authority with which patients could identify.

Negative identifications with roles considered improper and undesirable by the community were more prominent among class V than class III patients, since class V living conditions provided poor bases for positive identities. Society's very treatment of lower-class patients as "bad," "inferior," "dull," etc., also might have led them to choose a negative identity and become exactly what the community expected them to be, persons who aggressively "acted out" their hostility in antisocial and delinquent behavior.

Diagnostic Differences

The differential experiences of schizophrenic and neurotic patients seemed to reflect the importance of adequate adult identification figures for the individual's ego development. Significantly more fathers of schizophrenic than neurotic patients in both classes provided unsatisfactory models for the patients' behavior and ego ideals. These inadequate, passive, and withdrawn men did not seem to provide suitable identification objects for the development of the male schizophrenics' masculinity. When we also recognize the dependency of the male schizophrenics upon their mothers, it is not strange that most had serious problems in the performance of their adult social-sexual role. The consequences of this deficiency appeared greater in class V where male patients more frequently than in class III had to play an extremely aggressive masculine role to be successful. The fathers' role model provided female patients with a distorted view of the masculine adult role. Their mothers performed many family functions usually expected of a man, so the feminine model they presented was distorted as well. Problems of identification were intensified for the schizophrenic patients because of their cold and distant relationships with their fathers.

In general, schizophrenics more than neurotics were isolated from close parental relationships and were unable to identify in childhood with adequate adult figures. They were lonely and isolated, apparently finding it easier than most other people to give up their personal identity rather than adjust to the harsh realities of their environment.

It was interesting that many of the identification problems of class III schizophrenics were similar to those of neurotics as well as schizophrenics in class V. Nearly all class V patients in our study had identification problems similar to schizophrenics and they made similar, although less extreme, adjustments.

Life conditions in class V were such that one wonders why neurotics did not have even more serious problems of ego development. A clue to their better adjustment may have been the timely presence in their homes of adult relatives other than parents, since relatives such as aunts or grandmothers sometimes acted as parental surrogates in homes which were otherwise disorganized. Thus, the patients were not left entirely on their own or in the care of their brothers and sisters. Perhaps, these persons provided some stability in identification, even though of a temporary nature, for the class V neurotics.

SELECTED BIBLIOGRAPHY

DAGER, EDWARD Z., "Socialization and Personality Development in the Child," in Harold T. Christensen, ed., *Handbook of Marriage and the Family* (Chicago: Rand McNally & Co., 1964), pp. 740–81.

HOLLINGSHEAD, AUGUST B., and REDLICH, FREDERICK C., *Social Class and Mental Illness*. New York: John Wiley & Sons, Inc., 1958.

KAHL, JOSEPH A., *The American Class Structure*. New York: Holt, Rinehart & Winston, Inc., 1957.

KOHN, MELVIN L., "Social Class and Exercise of Parental Authority." *American Sociological Review* (June, 1959), pp. 352–66.

PARSONS, TALCOTT, and BALES, ROBERT F., *Family, Socialization and Interaction Process*. New York: Free Press of Glencoe, 1955.

WARNER, LLOYD W., MEEKER, MARCHIA, and EELLS, KENNETH, *Social Class in America*. New York: Harper & Row, Publishers, 1960.

THE WORLD OF THE FORMERLY MARRIED

Morton M. Hunt

The prevalent attitude today toward divorce and the divorced person is one of social confusion. The general social view of divorce tends to reflect the legal one—that one party is guilty and the other party innocent. To be the guilty party often means that one is viewed with social criticism; and so, frequently both parties attempt to place the blame for the divorce on the partner. The divorced person may feel that the only way for him to achieve social acceptance is to make it appear that the divorced partner was the one in the wrong. This may be seen as helping him not only to rationalize the divorce but to "explain" his error of falling in love with that person in the first place. This point is an important one because, with mate selection being currently the province of the individual, each individual must assume the responsibility for the error of his choice when it proves to be one that is so poor as to require divorce.

All divorced persons are faced with a realization that they have failed in their marriage and in their role as husband or wife. What may make this particularly difficult for some to accept is that the majority of married people do not feel compelled to end their marriages by divorce. Therefore, the divorced person may feel that he has been unable to succeed where the majority have succeeded. Many divorced people probably do not view their divorces as personal failures, but they may honestly feel they made mistakes in mate selection. Some may attempt to rationalize the situation by arguing that most marriages that remain intact are really unhappy and unsatisfactory. Because of the high American divorce rate, the divorced population is rapidly increasing; and, as it increases, those entering divorce will find it easier to justify their situations by identifying with this reference group. Both the increasing number of divorces and the related changing attitudes toward divorce may make the divorced person less subject to social stigma.

The confusion that exists regarding divorce is not just social confusion. There also may be personal confusion—a conflict or ambiguity of feelings for the couple or individual being divorced. The loss of the marriage partner and the end of the marriage relationship are both personal losses, and it is natural that the individual after divorce often feels a personal confusion. And the individual's feelings toward his divorced status will often have a strong influence on the way he will perform his new role of being divorced. For example, if the divorced woman is extremely bitter toward her ex-husband, her attitudes may influence her relationships with other males, restricting or inhibiting her sexual relationships. But, on the other hand, if she were able to see her divorced status as a step forward from the past marital status, her attitude might have a positive influence on her adjustment to her new role as a divorced person.

The majority of divorced people believe that the best possible adjustment to divorce is remarriage to a new partner. They feel that this provides them with an opportunity both personally and

socially to "right the wrong" of the previous marriage. In the selection that follows, Morton Hunt discusses the great importance of remarriage to the divorced and how they move back into marriage.

This study by Hunt represents a somewhat different approach from that of other selections in this book. He brings together his knowledge as a social scientist with his abilities as a trained and highly skilled writer. The result is a well written and perceptive account of the world of the divorced. (Although his work is titled THE WORLD OF THE FORMERLY MARRIED, he does not include the widowed.) Hunt's study centers mainly around the upper middle class. He used several different research techniques in his study. First, he lived among the divorced as a participant observer in the role of a divorced man; and this position allowed him to attend social functions and visit the homes and the favorite hangouts of the divorced in various parts of the United States. Second, he interviewed about 200 separated or divorced persons in the United States. Third, he developed a questionnaire of almost 150 items, which was answered by 169 adults of different age, religious, and educational levels scattered around the United States. The overall result of combining these different approaches provides a descriptive and insightful picture of the world of the divorced.

I. THE MARRYING KIND

In the first throes of loneliness, most FMs [Formerly Marrieds] see remarriage as the only possible solution, while later on, having discovered the compensations and privileges available within the World of the Formerly Married, they may be tempted to remain there indefinitely. Yet that world is not so much a substitute for marriage as a training ground for remarriage. Two generations ago, when this subculture scarcely existed, or existed in far less developed form, only one out of every three divorced people ever remarried;

today, although the FM's life has become easier and socially more acceptable, six out of seven do so. Despite the possibilities of comfortable long-term adjustment to divorced life, remarriage still seems to most FMs the best solution to their problems.

We have already observed the social pressures—estrangement from married friends, alienation from most social activities, an ambiguous and isolated position in the community—that motivate FMs to commit themselves to remarriage. Yet almost no one ever remarries primarily for such reasons; at least, it hardly ever feels that way. For these are "sensible" and practical considerations, and Americans feel it improper to marry on that basis. Even the divorcee who desperately needs financial support would feel she was selling herself if she married only for security; even the father with custody, who urgently needs someone to run his home and mother his children, has to feel another and nobler motive before making some woman his wife.

And that, of course, is Love—the one reason for remarrying in which all can take pride. Even though ours has been described as the Age of Cool, love is still the *sine qua non*, the major motive for remarrying. And marriage, in return, is the *sine qua non* of love; we live not in close-knit communities or large families, but in closely packed isolation; the only sure source of comfort, companionship, and love is one's spouse. As time passes, therefore, and the FM becomes better able to function sexually and emotionally within the World of the Formerly Married, he or she also becomes readier to attempt to satisfy deeper needs through marriage.

Most of the Formerly Married are not only capable of such a relationship, but have an innate preference for it rather than for the limited and casual kind. Despite previous marital failures, FMs remain marrying people: at every age level they are more likely to marry than people who have never been married at all, and this difference becomes greater as the age levels progress. Ninety-nine out of one hundred women who are divorced by twenty-five will remarry sooner or later; only eighty-eight out of one hundred single women of that same age will ever marry. Two out of three divorcees who are forty will eventually remarry, but only one out of seven single women of forty will do so. The odds favoring marriage are higher for both single and formerly married men at every age, but show a similar divergence.

All of which indicates that FMs and never-married people tend to have somewhat different kinds of personality—the more so as time filters and separates them. Except for the very young, most never-married people either do not need or cannot tolerate the intimacy of married love; FMs, despite the failure of their marriages, do need such intimacy, and either can tolerate it or mean to try their best. Nearly all FMs did love their mates for a while, even if imperfectly, and were loved in return; knowing something of that experience, they remain unsatisfied by the substitutes and the partial loves of unmarried life. For most of them, the mistake was not marriage itself but the particular marriage they made; only the "loners" were, at heart, non-marrying people who misjudged themselves and then learned better.

Yet few of the divorced are either clear or consistent about the kind of person they now believe they need and can love well enough to marry. Some think they know the traits they are searching for, but most are much more specific about the traits they want to avoid. Some are more exacting in their requirements than they were before; others are less so, and expect to find and tolerate many imperfections in anyone they love. Young and middle-aged FMs dwell upon the emotional and sexual characteristics they hope to find in a new mate; older FMs more often say they want someone companionable and easy to get along with. Nearly all believe they know themselves better now, and have a clearer notion of what sort of person they need; virtually all mean to avoid the sort they chose before.

Whatever it is they are seeking, formerly married people far more often find it among other FMs than among never-married or widowed persons. Divorced people marry other divorced people about sixty per cent of the time, single and widowed people only forty per cent of the time. But their preference for each other is even stronger than these figures indicate, for the proportion of FMs among the people from whom they are free to choose is less than half as large as the proportion they marry. To put it another way, since divorced women make up approximately one fourth of the total population of unmarried women from among whom divorced men are free to choose new mates, one might expect about one out of four remarrying men to select an FM woman and the other three to select single women or widows. But similarity of experience and social status draw FMs to one another so powerfully that divorced men actually marry divorced women two and a half times as often as chance or random choice would account for.

To the divorced person, another divorced person is knowable, familiar and, in a sense, dependable: the broken previous marriage is taken as an earnest of his or her intent to have an unbroken one, the wreckage of love is proof that love existed and can be rebuilt. The customs and social mechanisms of the World of the Formerly Married not only maximize the exposure of the divorced to other divorced people, but help them ready themselves to try to make good those hopes and promises.

II. RETURN TRIP

The course of true love never did run smooth and, as we have seen, it is especially bumpy for the Formerly Married. Unlike the young, who come to each other relatively empty-handed, the divorced man and divorced woman come with all the acquisitions of the years—their individual histories, habits, and tastes, their children, friends, and chattels. Love can be a rickety vehicle, loaded with so much of life's baggage, and the trip back to the world of the married is often interrupted by slow-downs, halts, and backsliding.

Nor is the way itself well-marked. Young unmarried people of the middle class follow a well-established route whose signposts are, usually, dating and necking, petting, going steady, talking about marriage, heavy petting or intercourse, formal engagement and, finally, marriage. FMs ignore this orderly progression: they rarely linger for any time at the dating and necking stage, but proceed swiftly to full sexual relations—in advance of most of the development of feelings of love. As for marriage, the woman very likely thinks secretly about the possibility of it the first time they make love, much as she did in any previous affairs; the man may refuse to let himself do so that soon, or may think about it but wrestle the thought into submission. Yet if it is an affair with marriage potential, both of them openly begin to refer to it far sooner than unmarried people would, but usually in a bantering manner; humor keeps the subject from being alarming. He may, for instance, grumble that what will finally force him to get married again is the pain of getting up in the middle of the night and dressing to go home; she may retort that for her it is the need to have someone who can open stuck windows.

And soon they deliberately act the part of man and wife without discussing it—they may pile his children and hers in the car for a day at the beach, and play the father and mother for each other's benefit even more than that of the youngsters. Or perhaps he will come over for dinner one evening, wearing old clothes, in order to fix things for her—a couple of doors that will not close, a lamp that needs rewiring; seeing him do this with her two excited boys as helpers, she glows, feels protected, and is filled with affection. Or perhaps they spend a Sunday afternoon together reading the paper and loafing, and later leave the children with a baby-sitter and visit friends for the evening. "Pretty domestic kind of day, wasn't it?" he says—and abruptly switches to some other subject; but both of them know he liked the thought more than he feared it.

The unmarried, having never been man or wife to anyone, may need signs and symbols to mark their progress; the Formerly Married mark theirs instead by ever more daringly testing out the roles of man and wife. Yet many of them omit the conventional gestures of courtship: half of those who finally remarry do so without ever having announced an engagement, and even those who do have an engagement announce it more quietly and keep it briefer than do the never-married. In part this probably reflects the greater experience and more realistic outlook of the Formerly Married: they have been through one or more affairs already that have fallen short, and know how many complications there are in their lives, how many possibilities exist for disagreement or disenchantment, how many habits and tastes they must try out on each other, how many situations they need to see each other in before committing themselves and their children to what they hope will be a permanent relationship.

Even after they have begun to love each other in earnest, and to feel genuinely committed, any one of a hundred difficulties may make them suddenly waver and briefly doubt that it can ever work. Perhaps at first he likes her children, but later becomes jealous of them, or impatient or too stern; he and she argue about it for hours; then, growing gentle and sad, they hold hands and talk long and softly about whether or not they are wrong for each other. Or perhaps she seemed soft, womanly, and gentle at first, but later shows a strength and obstinacy that exasperate him; after a series of angry interchanges, they fall silent until she comes over to him, tender and contrite, and they cling to each other like weary swimmers to a float; they kiss and forgive, but each wonders whether they have solved the problem or only postponed facing it squarely. Or perhaps he has a series of business problems, and is preoccupied and impatient; she tries to understand, but needs more of him than he is giving her, says as much, and instead of making him warmer and more attentive only makes him feel guilty and angry.

Yet in the love affair which does proceed toward marriage, these problems are resolved in one way or another, and love grows. For some, that growth is relatively easy and spontaneous; for most, it requires a great deal of work. Perhaps she is ready to be reassured of his affection five minutes after a spat, while he needs an hour or two to simmer down; either one or both of them must change, or they must get used to their differences and learn to allow for them. Perhaps she chokes back anger and fumes quietly, when he has hurt her feelings; he may have to draw her out, make her talk, and teach her to discuss it with him rather than bottle it up. Each finds innumerable ways to please the other a little with certain words, special smiles, tiny deeds. Each learns which things they both like and can enjoy together, and which they must let each other enjoy alone. Each makes dozens of compromises and bargains with the other about their tastes in food and sex, their ways with children, their needs in friends.

Unmarried young people go steady but continue to act like dates who are in love; the Formerly Married go together and act like lovers who have just been married. Dating becomes a thing of the past; they evolve into a couple, seeing each other as much as they can, growing so comfortable that they can sit quietly in the same room, reading and not feeling obliged to talk. But they do talk a great deal: each is eager to share with the other the experiences of the day, each devours the other's words so as to live the other's life vicariously. Waking or sleeping, working or playing, in each other's presence or apart, they become intertwined and enmeshed, until they are no longer lonely when alone, no longer single when solitary.

And now a change in allegiances comes about almost by itself. They meet or visit married friends, and find them indulgent, warm, approving; the married people welcome them with a slightly annoying largeness of spirit, as though they had strayed from the True Church and now are penitently returning. At the same time they are beginning to feel themselves drawing away from their FM friends; it is not a matter of a deliberately created distance, but of an inevitable decrease in the number of shared feelings, a loss of identification, a regrowth of privacy. If the man still has a couple of drinks or spends an evening with another formerly married male, or the woman meets another divorcee for lunch, each smiles and talks as always, but something is different; an inner barrier, invisible but almost tangible, separates them and blocks out certain confidences and intimacies. For they no longer want to share their intimate feelings with others, now that they love. The same man who could talk volubly to a friend about a sexual fling or even a new and promising affair can hardly bring himself to say that he feels a deeper and richer love now than ever before; instead he relies on simple clichés: "I think this is really it" or "This one's different."

It is at once marvelous to feel one's self rejoining all that from which one had felt alienated, and rather sad to feel one's self becoming alienated from all that to which one had been joined. Like seniors at graduation, the lover and his FM friends are effusive when they meet but ill-at-ease; already it is clear they are going different ways, that each is holding back part of himself and guarding some of his thoughts while pretending to pour them out freely. They know with regret that the promises of continuing friendship are well-meant, but that the friendship will not continue as it was. The FMs are glad for the lovers but a little jealous; they wish the lovers well, but feel almost deserted, almost betrayed.

Somehow the word is finally given out—perhaps in the form of an informal, verbally announced engagement, perhaps merely in the form of a casual mention to friends about a wedding date. It is at this very point that some FMs suddenly become alarmed at the multiplicity of adjustments they will have to make in the future, or belatedly discover some seemingly insoluble problem in the marriage they had planned. One or the other of them may grow panicky and call a halt to everything, postponing the wedding indefinitely; then the panic recedes, they rush together again, the wavering one is forgiven, the plans are renewed. Despite shilly-shallying, they move rapidly toward their goal and arrive there soon: FMs spend less than half the time in courtship that never-married people do. For though the Formerly Married have so many bits and pieces to fit together, they are adept and knowing about it; moreover, being adult, they are impatient to live within marriage again, and not content to play at it from the remoteness of engagement.

Many an FM is apprehensive when the time comes to tell the children about the future marriage, and with good reason. No matter how eagerly children had besought their parent to remarry, their ambivalence usually became obvious as the courtship progressed. The more absorbed the man and woman became in each other, the more rivalry the children showed, even though they also showed increasing fondness and trust. In view of their conflicting feelings, one never knows in advance just how they will respond to the news. Small children may burst into happy tears, or they may have a tantrum; older ones may be warmly congratulatory, or outspokenly critical and cold. Strong reactions of one sort or another are more likely on the part of the woman's children; happily, they are positive more often than not. In the case of the man's children, the limited amount of contact they have with their father and his daily life tends to make their reactions milder; they are about as likely to be indifferent as delighted, and are only rarely hostile or upset.

The wedding is usually far simpler than the ceremonies of people marrying for the first time. Only about half of the remarriages are held in churches, as compared with four fifths of first marriages. The bride does not wear white, and rarely wears a long gown; she appears usually in a cocktail dress or even sometimes a suit. The minister, rabbi, or officiating justice keeps the ceremony short, and eliminates from his customary wedding speech the glowing promises that have already once proven false for both bride and groom. Even the cake, if there is one, is plain; a bakery in New York has, for instance, tactfully designed a special model for remarriages, featuring white sugar bells on top in place of the usual figures of bride and groom. Offsetting these simplifications are a few special complexities: children of both sides underfoot, excited and noisy; relatives and old friends who have known bride or groom in the previous marriage, and who have to exercise special care not to say anything inappropriate; married friends and FMs, an occasional ex-in-law or ex-lover, sometimes even an ex-spouse, all intermingling, putting on their best smiles, and trying to take each other's measure; and throughout, amidst the prevailing atmosphere of good will and good wishes, the unspoken, almost palpable thought in the minds of most of those present: "I hope it works out this time"—at once a wish and a doubt. Then it is over. The newly married people have left the World of the Formerly Married; they are no longer rebels, dissidents, non-conformists; they have rejoined the flock and made peace with their society.

III. WILL IT WORK?

What chance is there that this remarriage, or remarriages in general, will do well? It is a subject about which experts have widely differing opinions.

A number of psychoanalysts, marriage counsellors, and psychotherapists whose views derive from Freudian psychology hold that human personality is formed in its essentials by childhood experiences, and is not capable of significant change in adulthood except through deep psychotherapy; they therefore feel that the experiences of marriage, divorce, and life as an FM cannot modify the individual in any important sense, and that in remarriage he will only make the same mistakes and encounter the old problems again.

One of the best-known exponents of this view was the late Edmund Bergler, a psychoanalyst who set forth his opinions in a book entitled *Divorce Won't Help.* Dr. Bergler stated that divorcing people believe they have learned a lot from their mistakes and are sure they will be more successful in their next marriage, but that this is pure illusion; they are wholly unaware of the actual reasons for their choice of the wrong partner, their behavior within marriage, and their decision to flee via divorce. For these reasons, which are part of their neuroses, are thoroughly hidden in the unconscious; and since adult experiences do not modify the individual's neurosis, divorced people are bound to fall in love unwisely again, and to fail again in marriage. "Since the neurotic is unconsciously always on the lookout for his complementary neurotic type," wrote Dr. Bergler, "the chances of finding conscious happiness in the next marriage are exactly zero. . . . The second, third, and *n*th marriages are but repetitions of previous experiences."

On the other hand, a growing number of psychoanalysts

and clinical psychologists believe that human nature remains much more plastic after childhood than Freud realized, and that it is capable of change and growth even in the adult years, if exposed to significant experiences or to a new environment. It follows that marriage, divorce, and FM life can importantly add to the individual's emotional capacity, self-knowledge, and judgment, and that most divorced people should do better in their remarriages than they did in their first ones. Apart from psychological grounds for such a belief, a number of sociologists hold that the statistics on remarriage indicate that faulty first marriages must be not so much the result of neurosis as of normal errors, misjudgments, and incompatibilities. The late Dr. Abraham Stone, an expert on sexual problems and a marriage counsellor of vast experience, concluded from his own observations that "the majority of bad marriages are those in which the individuals are quite normal and average, but are wrong for one another, though each might have been right for somebody else." Professor Jessie Bernard found in her own extensive study of remarried persons that the majority of divorces are caused by "team factors"—normal misjudgments, based on inexperience, as to how two given personalities will fit together in the partnership of marriage. "The experience of an unhappy first marriage," she writes, "although it may constitute a high tuition fee, may nevertheless serve as a valuable educational prerequisite to a successful second marriage."

"Who shall decide, when doctors disagree?" Perhaps the divorced themselves; at least they should know whether they are making the same mistakes, even if they fail to understand why.

A certain number of FMs do admit that they are still often attracted by the same type of persons they were married to, but claim that they hastily back away as soon as they recognize the similarity. Others take longer, and get themselves into trouble. One man writes that he fell in love with and married a pretty little girl whose tart tongue and witty manner delighted him; as her husband, however, he found that she was a belittling and hostile woman. After divorce, he tried to avoid her type, and eventually became involved with a tall, earnestly intellectual college instructor; it took several months before he realized that he had changed only the unessentials; she often used her intellectuality to express the same kind of hostility toward him, and toward all men, as had his first wife. He got out of the affair with some difficulty, and probably saved himself the pain of a second divorce.

A few FMs admit that they did not see the similarities soon enough and ended up, as Dr. Bergler said they would, with the same unhappy results. A young businesswoman who was married to an architect for four years, and to an industrial designer for two, explains:

I did the same thing in my second marriage that I had the first time—I chose someone insecure and undeveloped, and tried to make him mature. Believe it or not, I actually financed *both* of these men all the way through their graduate education. I played mother and teacher and big sister to each of them. It works fine but only for a while; then I get frustrated, because I want somebody to lean on, and they get difficult because they don't want to grow up. I finally went into psychotherapy, and once I understood that the problem was of my own making, I never let myself make the mistake again.

But without requiring psychotherapy, most divorced people seem determined to avoid the same kind of relationship they had the first time. Some say they still feel a certain pull toward the same type of person but have learned to recognize and deny the impulse, and to react more positively to quite different types. Others find themselves actually repelled by the traits they once liked. A forty-five-year-old securities analyst speaks:

My first wife was a real bohemian—zany, sloppy, always going off on the spur of the moment and leaving things on the stove to burn up, spending more than we had on a wild impulse to fly to Mexico—things like that. It seemed exciting and magical when I was twenty-five, but after six years of it and a divorce I found it loathsome. Instead, I found myself liking other kinds of people with qualities I used to sneer at. My present wife is sensible and competent and even-tempered. She loves fun but has a sense of responsibility to me and the children.

Though such testimony does not constitute rigorous proof, it does suggest that many of the Formerly Married have learned to avoid choosing the same sort of person they were married to before. Yet this is no absolute guarantee that they will do better in a second marriage. The all-important question remains: Is the chance of happiness in the second marriage "exactly zero," or is it reasonably good?

One kind of evidence often brought to bear on this point is the divorce rate of the remarried. A few studies of this rate have been made at various times in different parts of the country; the figures differ somewhat, but are always higher than those for first marriages. One of the most recent and careful studies, based on Iowa records for the early 1950's, shows that remarriages are twice as likely to break up as first marriages. Those who marry a third or subsequent time run a still greater risk of further divorce: if both spouses have been divorced twice or more, the chance of a later marriage failing is nearly five times as great as it is for a first marriage.

Such figures are often used as proof that divorced people lack the capacity to make successful marriages, and are bound to fail again and again. But this conclusion is unwarranted. At least sixty per cent of second marriages do endure until death. Moreover, some divorce-prone people become chronic repeaters and reappear again and again in the remarriage and divorce data, making the chance of divorce for the mass of remarrying FMs look greater than it actually is.

But even those who do get divorced a second time are not all neurotics and marital incompetents. Some—perhaps even most—are acting upon what they have learned: that divorce is not as dreadful as they had once thought; that the life of the FM is not necessarily unhappy or unrewarding; and that even the distressing aspects of divorce are less destructive of the personality than remaining in a bad marriage. Their second divorces do not show an inability ever to make a successful marriage; they do show an increasing readiness to give up an unsuccessful one.

Another kind of evidence is the survey in which remarried people, or people who know them, are asked to evaluate the happiness of their second marriages. Of the handful of such studies, the two most important are in close agreement, even though they used different methods and were based on people in different parts of the country. Psychologist Harvey J. Locke, in his book *Predicting Adjustment in Marriage,* presented the results of his survey of 146 chiefly middle-class people, all remarried, some of whom lived in Indiana and some in California. He found three-quarters of them to be happy or very happy, and only one out of nine unhappy or very unhappy; the remainder lay in between. Dr. Jessie Bernard based her study, *Remarriage,* on some two thousand middle- and upper-middle-class remarriages in a Northeastern state, two-thirds of which involved at least one FM, the other partners being widowed or never-married persons; these marriages were evaluated for her not by themselves but by others. Seven-eighths of them were rated anywhere from satisfactory to extremely satisfactory; only one-eighth were said to be unsatisfactory or extremely unsatisfactory.

Although neither of these researchers asked how the second marriage compared with the first, the answer would seem perfectly obvious; nevertheless, Dr. William Goode, as part of his study, *After Divorce,* asked that question of all the remarried women in his sample. Nearly ninety per cent considered their second marriages much better than their first ones; the rest found them only a little better, or no better, or worse. Dr. Goode cautiously points out that all of these women had been remarried two years or less, and may have been somewhat more enthusiastic than they will be later on; even allowing for this, however, the evidence strongly contradicts the opinion of Dr. Bergler and his allies that the remarried are bound to fail again and that their chances of doing better the second time are nil.

So much for the bare bones of statistics—but how does it feel in the flesh? Even if a majority do better the second time, is the difference great enough to warrant all that they had to go through? Three remarried people—one unhappy, one moderately happy, and one very happy—may help us decide for ourselves. First, a Midwestern business executive, now forty-eight, represents those who are unhappy the second time around:

I married my second wife on the rebound when I wasn't ready for matrimony, and ruined all my hopes of a better life by picking even more poorly than I did the first time. For these past six years, I've been trying far harder to make a go of it than she is willing to make. She turned out to be a lousy housekeeper, which bothers me no end since I am compulsively neat. She is continually dissatisfied with her lot, and accuses me all the time of either holding money back from her or not earning enough to provide properly for her and our children, even though I make nearly $20,000 a year. The worst thing is that she got the German measles when she was pregnant with our second child, and though I begged her to get a legal abortion, she refused, and gave birth to a Mongolian defective. Since then her shrewishness has been unbearable. I can't think how to improve the situation. She won't consider marriage counselling. There is no real communication, and what love we had once is completely soured. But if I can't salvage this marriage, and have to go through divorce again, I will feel really like a hopeless case. In fact, I feel like one right now.

Next, a striking redhead of thirty-four, brisk and saucy in manner and a highly efficient personal secretary, represents the great majority who consider their remarriages average or somewhat above average in happiness:

Tony isn't an ideal husband—that's an understatement. He can be a damned difficult man when his writing isn't going well—sullen, nasty, unwilling to do anything around the house, drinking too much, sitting up all hours and smoking, sometimes going out without saying a word and staying out until I'm worried sick. And in any kind of crisis he's no help at all—when the maid doesn't show up, for instance, or the landlord won't come fix the furnace, you'd think it was the end of the world. But he's got a fabulous mind, and when things are going well he's funny and kind and gay. In fact, even when he's being difficult he's never dull. And he's masculine through and through. I never feel the lack of that, as I did with my first. He's a pretty good father, at least when he's in a good mood. All in all, it's not as good a marriage as I myself once hoped for, and promised myself to make, but I think it's at least as good as most. Maybe better. I'm not complaining.

Finally, there are the minority whose remarriages are extremely satisfactory or very happy; a woman in her early forties who teaches history in a small New England college can serve as a model of this group:

My first marriage was sociologically ideal—similar backgrounds, income level, tastes, education: all the factors were beautifully matched. But we were friendly strangers from the beginning. He was always unromantic, cool, fair-minded, rational, but he was never really involved with me as a human being, and he became less and less so as time passed and his business interests multiplied. It was a very smooth organization that we ran and called a marriage. We didn't have fights that wasn't the trouble—it was just that there was nothing happening between us. Even when he finally came home from his many activities for a weekend, he wanted to sleep and rest, and read in bed, and be left alone. There was no companionship, no communication, little sex. I felt unimportant and purposeless—and I thought all marriages were like that after the honeymoon period. But in contrast, my present husband, though he is a whirlwind and a hard worker—he's a gynecologist—is warm and intense, and I come first in his life and he in mine. It is more beautiful and exciting after four years than I could have imagined. We spend every possible moment together because we want to. We have travelled to Asia and Australia together, lectured together, cleaned the barn and hunted and fished and skiied together; we sleep rolled in one tight ball together. Each of us wants to make the other feel secure in our love. Ours is a genuine *union*.

Not many remarriages—and not many first marriages, for that matter—can match this one; yet a considerable number of those who do have successful remarriages speak, with some of the same sense of wonder, of the discovery of a more satisfying and different kind of love. Such people would have no trouble at all answering the question as to whether there is enough difference between the first marriage and the second to warrant all that they had to go through; in fact, the question might strike them as somewhat absurd.

IV. IS IT WORTH IT?

But however emphatically the question might be answered for themselves by the very happily remarried, or even by those who have achieved only an average degree of happiness, we need to ask it in another and broader sense: Is divorce, generally speaking, a morally valid choice—that is, by and large does it do more evil than good, or more good than evil, to all concerned than remaining in an unhappy marriage? For non-divorce, like divorce, involves a host of consequences for man and wife, for children, and for society; and since these may be either healthful or noxious, it can be morally as bad or as good a choice as divorce itself.

Let us, therefore, consider non-divorce for a moment. Almost no one will take issue with the premise that if poor marriages could, of themselves, turn into good ones, or be remade into good ones by outside influences, non-divorce would be the preferable alternative—definitely so where there are children, marginally so where there are not. What, then, is the likelihood that improvement in a poor marriage will take place spontaneously? Folk wisdom tells of the newly married couple's "period of adjustment," during which all sorts of conflicts and difficulties are ironed out until marital happiness succeeds the post-honeymoon let-down. There is at least some sociological evidence to back up this popular belief. Professor Judson T. Landis once studied 409 long-term marriages and found that in six major activities of married life (friendships, finances, sex, and so on) anywhere from one quarter to one half of the husbands and wives felt there had been maladjustment at the outset; in each of the six activities, about half of these people felt that they had arrived at a state of adjustment with their spouses, the time this took ranging anywhere from several months to many years.

But this is less encouraging than it sounds. It is one thing for two compatible, but new, partners in marriage to have their initial maladjustments dissolved by familiarity and time; it is quite another thing, and far less likely, for there to be a spontaneous remission of any severe, deep-rooted conflicts that emerge as two people come to know each other intimately. Ersel E. LeMasters, director of the School of Social Work at the University of Wisconsin, studied a group of marriages which had had serious conflicts in them for a number of years; later on, he did a follow-up and found that although only one-fifth of them had broken up, not one of the four-fifths that remained intact had improved by itself. In most of these intact marriages, furthermore, one or both spouses were paying heavy penalties in the form of alcoholism, psychosomatic disorders, neurosis, work troubles, depression, and the like. Many other studies of troubled marriages made by caseworkers and other experts in family life have reached the same conclusions: the spontaneous improvement of marriages with profound conflict is extremely rare, and continued living in such a marriage can be seriously damaging to the personality of one or both spouses.

If there is little hope of spontaneous improvement, what are the chances that a disintegrating marriage can be held together and made into a good one by means of outside help? It is a truism among marriage counsellors, as among psychotherapists in general, that the patient has very little chance of improvement unless he wants to get better, but the vast majority of people who have reached the point of openly considering divorce do not want to be reconciled. In Wayne County, Michigan, which includes Detroit and its environs, an agency called "The Friend of the Court" offers marriage counselling to every divorcing couple that wants it, but although 11,000 couples filed for divorce in 1965, only 401 of them accepted the offer of counselling; about one quarter of these couples were reconciled. A somewhat better success record has been compiled by the Conciliation Court of Los Angeles County, which manages to work out reconciliations, through counselling, for a little over half of those couples where both partners voluntarily enter into the process. But in recent years, even though these services have become more popular, only between four and six per cent of the couples filing for divorce in Los Angeles County have been using the Court; the net result is that the salvage rate of all dissolving marriages is still very small. A compulsory reconciliation service, like that just enacted into New York's new divorce law, may force a great many people to confer with the counsellors, but it is very doubtful that this will save any large percentage of marriages. Even working with motivated voluntary clients, marriage counsellors throughout the country report significant improvement in less than half the cases; with unmotivated and unwilling clients, the rate of success is bound to be much smaller. Marriage counselling, though it can often heal a sick marriage, has little chance of saving a dying one and almost no chance of bringing a dead one back to life.

It would seem, then, that in the great majority of cases where marriage has become thoroughly unsatisfying, or is racked by deep emotional conflict, non-divorce is unlikely to result in happy marriage. Yet this is not the same as saying that divorce is necessarily a more successful alternative. To find out whether it is or not, let us turn again to the evidence.

The success or failure of divorce, first of all, does not depend solely on whether or not it leads to a new and happier marriage. We have seen that marital dissolution can of itself have results ranging anywhere from the profoundly beneficial to the profoundly harmful. At one extreme, an unremarried divorcee says that she is "surrounded by the wreckage of all that meant anything to her" and is unable ever to care for, or to trust in, anyone again; at the other extreme, an unremarried man says that divorce has brought him "terrible years but wonderful years, a second chance at life, a wholly new outlook on myself and the people around me. I shudder to think that I might have lived out my life without all this happening to me."

Thus, even among unremarried FMs, we can distinguish between the successfully and the unsuccessfully divorced. What we have seen indicates that the unsuccessful ones constitute a small minority of FMs, and the very successful a somewhat larger minority; in between, the great majority are reasonably successful. Most of the latter will not consider themselves wholly successful until they remarry, yet most of them feel they are better off than they were and have no regrets about the divorce. Four-fifths of Dr. Goode's sample, for instance, apparently had no reservations about the wisdom of their choice, since they felt that if they had stayed married, their marriages would only have deteriorated further, or at best shown no improvement.

Beyond this, however, people do very commonly weigh the outcome of divorce in terms of remarriage. The success of divorce, so judged, is not overwhelming, but it is at least respectable; as we have just seen, except for the severely neurotic and other special types, most of the Formerly Married have an even chance, or better, of achieving a satisfactory second marriage, and a very good chance of achieving one that is an improvement over the first. For the great majority of them, that is success enough.

The divorcing persons themselves are not, of course, the only ones whose lives are affected by their choice. Children are involved in sixty per cent of today's divorces, and it has long been standard for those who write about divorce to deplore the damage done to the children by the shattering of family life. Quite a few years ago, some of those who were scandalized by the climbing divorce rate pointed with horror to the very high proportion—sometimes said to be as high as eighty per cent—of delinquent children who came from broken homes; even today the bald assertion that divorce causes delinquency is still repeated, usually by opponents of divorce-law liberalization. But more searching analyses have suggested a larger cause associated with both divorce and delinquency—namely, social and economic deprivation: divorce and delinquency are both more common among poorer people, and occur side-by-side, perhaps not so much as cause-and-effect as two effects of the same general cause.

One way to prove this would be to compare the delinquency rates from intact and broken homes at the same economic level. Sheldon and Eleanor Glueck, in their careful study, *Unraveling*

Juvenile Delinquency, attempted to do just this—they studied children from intact and broken homes in the same neighborhoods. They did find some degree of connection between the broken homes and delinquency, but it was very much smaller than had been supposed: within this one stratum of society, not eighty but only twenty-one per cent of delinquents came from homes where the parents were separated or divorced. A somewhat larger proportion of delinquent children came from broken homes than from unbroken ones, but this difference could not be ascribed solely to the fact that the family had split up: although the Gluecks had drawn upon homes in the same or similar neighborhoods, they found that economic and physical conditions in the broken homes were quite a bit worse than those in the intact homes; those conditions may have been partly responsible for the difference in the delinquency rate. A number of other investigations of the subject have shown that the delinquency rates for children from broken and unbroken homes are not very far apart; and even where there are definite differences in the rates, those differences are not greater than one might expect on the basis of pre-existing economic or psychological inferiority of the broken homes. One may reasonably conclude that divorce is responsible only to a limited extent for delinquency.

But even if divorce is far less likely to result in delinquency than has been alleged, perhaps it does produce other forms of damage to the personality. Nearly all FMs are deeply concerned over the harm they feel sure divorce must do to their children, and very often these fears are confirmed by the symptoms they see in them at the time of separation and for a while thereafter: crying spells, guilt feelings, nightmares and bedwetting, sudden babyishness or aggressive playing, stammering, loss of interest in school, and many more. Longer-range effects are harder to identify, though they are said to include fearfulness about love and marriage, resentment toward men or toward women, and inability to relate to other people.

Putting aside for a moment the question of how frequent and how real such difficulties are, the crucial question is whether non-divorce would create fewer or more of them. The traditional view has long been that people should stay together, at least until the children grow up, on the assumption that this is far more healthful for them than divorce; conversely, people who do divorce are thought to be robbing their children of the benefits of a secure and happy childhood. But the testimony of nearly all the experts sharply contradicts these notions. Dr. J. Louise Despert, the author of *Children of Divorce* and a child psychiatrist who has had wide clinical experience with children both from divorced and from unhappy unbroken homes, says that "divorce is not automatically destructive to children; the marriage which divorce brings to an end may have been more so." Divorce, she says, may be "a cleansing and healing experience for the child." Other psychiatrists have found that the ending of a bad marriage seems to bring great relief to children; that it creates security and consistency in the family pattern, ending an intolerable vacillation in the children between hope and fear; and that it brings the child's fears of desertion out of the unconscious into the open, where he can finally learn to handle them.

To test such clinical impressions on a broad scale, F. Ivan Nye, a sociologist now at Florida State University, compared a large group of adolescents from broken homes with another large group from unhappy unbroken homes; the former turned out to be less often delinquent, better adjusted to their parents, and to have distinctly fewer psychosomatic ailments. Dr. Nye feels that this important phenomenon has been generally overlooked because family counsellors and child guidance workers focus their attention on the difficulties and tensions children experience at the time of the breakup; after a while, however, in a life free from the previous conflicts, the children adapt and reach a new equilibrium—but by that time no one is looking.

Divorce therefore seems preferable, from the viewpoint of the children's well-being, to the continuation of a seriously unhappy marriage. Nonetheless, many FMs continue to believe that in breaking up their marriages they have permanently harmed their children. Even if divorce is the less damaging alternative, the thought that they have done any damage at all makes them suffer from a continuing guilt. But how much actual damage have they done? Social scientists who have studied the children of divorce, seeing them without the distorting influence of guilt feelings, have found relatively little evidence of lasting emotional trauma due to the divorce itself. Children of divorce, and children living in intact and, for the most part, normal homes, have emotional problems in about the same numbers and degree of severity. In one of the most recent studies of the subject, published in 1964, Lee G. Burchinal, a professor of sociology at Iowa State University, gathered information about two large groups of seventh-grade and eleventh-grade students and compared those from intact homes with those from broken homes and homes where there had been a remarriage; he could find almost no difference among them.

What, then, of the effects of divorce outside the family itself? Does it or does it not do any harm to the society in which the divorcing people live? Most Western societies seem to think of it as potentially harmful; they regulate marriage and divorce, but maintain far more stringent controls over the latter than over the former. In the United States, whether people use a religious or civil marriage ceremony, the resulting union has the legal value of a private contract between two consenting parties, such as is made by people going into a business partnership; but while every one of the fifty states permits all other private contracts to be dissolved at the mutual wish of both parties involved, it does not do so in the case of marriage. This is the only form of private contract from which partners can be released only by permission of the state, which retains the right to decide whether dissolution is or is not justified.

The only valid ground for the state's interference in this private contract is its interest in the preservation of social order, which would presumably be threatened if any large number of children became dependent on the state, or delinquent, as a result of divorce. Those who oppose easier divorce laws often point out that even the Soviet Union, though it made marriage and divorce a personal matter after the Revolution, had to pull in the reins again by means of the family edict of July 8th, 1944, which put an end to the legal recognition of unregistered marriages and to easy divorce. The inference is that easy divorce had proven hurtful to social order in the U.S.S.R., and had to be eliminated. In actual fact, there is no evidence whatever that it did so; it was ended primarily because it conflicted with the Stalinist goal of population growth, for which family stability, rather than freedom to pursue happiness, seemed a necessary condition.

It is fairly well known that freedom to divorce has existed in certain deteriorating societies; this was the case in the later years of the Roman Empire. What is less well known, freedom to divorce has existed in certain stable and healthy societies—especially those which have mechanisms other than the father-mother family for insuring the well-being and socialization of the children. The Hopi Indians, and various other preliterate peoples, had very high divorce rates but without creating serious problems concerning child-rearing and socialization. Among the Hopi the married couple lived with the wife's family; if there was a divorce, the husband moved back to his mother's house, while the wife remained in a household with her relatives, where her children were cared for and educated without difficulty. Although this is a pattern more often seen in primitive societies, something analogous to it exists in the pioneer communities of Israel—the *kibbutzim*—where the effects of divorce on the children have been minimal because they live apart from the parents in children's quarters and are cared for by trained specialists.

"There is no reason to believe," writes Dr. Kingsley Davis, of the University of California, Berkeley, an eminent researcher of family and social problems, "that a highly tolerant attitude toward divorce in the United States will mean the decline and fall of our civilization. . . . The only necessity is that some sort of social machinery be worked out for rearing the child properly—a necessity hard to supply in our culture."

For the time being, we can only piece together makeshift machinery—the use of schools after hours, day care and playgroup facilities (both privately and publicly supported), cooperative nurseries, and the like. Yet even in advance of the fuller development of such devices and the creation of new ones, all those divorcing people who either can afford private facilities to aid them in the care and training of their children, or who have familial and other help with these tasks, may feel reasonably certain that they are not impairing the health of society. Indeed, if, as we have seen, their children would be somewhat more likely to grow up emotionally disturbed in an unbroken unhappy home, the decision to divorce is, even from society's standpoint, the better one.

Critics of divorce have raised the question of whether it is in conflict with the fundamental American way of life. They often see it as a repudiation of the American belief in family life, and a threat to moral values. They offer a number of alternatives: the conservatives among them urge acceptance of one's marriage, for the good of all concerned, the liberals stress the use of professional help to keep marriage intact, and a handful of radicals argue that freely condoned adultery will relieve the intolerable demands and tedium of monogamy. On one thing all three groups agree: the idealized romantic concept of marital love is a major reason for discontent and divorce; a more practical and down-to-earth view would be better for us all. But all these approaches to the divorce problem are, curiously, more impractical than the romantic notion of marriage, and more in conflict with the American philosophy of life than divorce itself.

Marriage, after all, is the only way Americans can find a great many of the emotional rewards they urgently need in life; to accept an unhappy marriage, to adjust to a loveless one, or to separate sex from marital love, is to ignore the most important benefits modern marriage has to offer, which are almost unobtainable elsewhere. In a world that has grown huge and impersonal, marriage is our principal source of emotional satisfaction, security, and individual happiness. Until society invents and perfects some new forms of grouping, some new kinds of attachment among people, we will need to have our marital partners be romantic as well as companionable, sexual as well as parental, exciting as well as domestic. This being so, we are right to be idealistic about marriage and to hope for much from it. We naturally rejoice greatly when it yields most of what we want, and cast it aside grievingly when it fails us.

And even if one agreed that it was foolish to hope for so much from marriage, is it not every man's right, in the United States, to commit follies in his pursuit of happiness? The meaning of the right to this pursuit has changed greatly since Jefferson first wrote it into the Declaration of Independence, but in recent decades the courts have more and more often equated it with both the freedom of contract and the freedom to labor, provided no harm is done to the rights of others. Divorce, as long as it does no harm, or at least less harm than continuation of a poor marriage, is clearly justified by this doctrine. The freedom to divorce is therefore a truly American right, which it is unjust to abridge by social or psychological pressure or by passing or maintaining restrictive laws.

It is for these reasons that divorce has become so common despite the existence of legal impediments. Between 1867 and 1960 the United States divorce rate increased more than sevenfold, even though the divorce laws of a number of states were made more stringent and conservative during that same period of time. If divorce were banned by law in all the states tomorrow, family life would be not better preserved; the deep needs and the basic philosophy of the people would lead them to disobey the law and live according to their consciences in illegal but satisfying unions, as is the case in Italy—a country without legal divorce—where some two and a half million people now live in such liaisons.

The wide use of divorce today is not a sign of a diminished desire to be married, but of an increased desire to be happily married. Never before in our history has marriage been more popular than it is today; in 1900 when, according to fond literary legend, everyone lived in warm familial contentment, only a little more than half of all men and women fourteen years old and over were married; today almost two-thirds are. More than ever, Americans want to marry well; more than ever they are willing to seek a good marriage, even if it means undergoing the long and often wretched experiences of divorce; more than ever they are coming to believe that divorce is morally justifiable in terms of the well-being of all concerned. For in the light of its consequences, divorce clearly appears to be a highly moral act, not only in many specific situations but in a broader sense. It is the necessary corollary of our elevated ideal of marriage, our valuation of emotional health, and our respect for the individual's right to seek happiness.

SELECTED BIBLIOGRAPHY

BERNARD, JESSIE, *Remarriage*. New York: Holt, Rinehart & Winston, Inc., 1956.

BOWERMAN, CHARLES, and IRISH, DONALD P., "Some Relationships of Step-children to Their Parents." *Marriage and Family Living* (May, 1962), pp. 113–21.

BURCHINAL, LEE G., "Characteristics of Adolescents from Unbroken, Broken, and Reconstituted Families." *Journal of Marriage and Family* (February, 1964), pp. 44–51.

DESPERT, J. LOUISE, *Children of Divorce*. New York: Doubleday & Company, Inc., 1953.

GOODE, WILLIAM J., *After Divorce*. New York: Free Press of Glencoe, 1956.

LANDIS, JUDSON T., "The Trauma of Children When Parents Divorce." *Marriage and Family Living* (February, 1960), pp. 7–13.

MONAHAN, THOMAS P., "The Duration of Marriage to Divorce: Second Marriages and Migratory Types." *Marriage and Family Living* (May, 1959), pp. 134–38.

NYE, F. IVAN, "Child Adjustment in Broken and in Unhappy Unbroken Homes." *Marriage and Family Living* (November, 1957), pp. 356–61.

INDEX

Kinsley's

Casters

LA

TAND

VOL I